The Pleistocene Social Contract

The Pleistocene Social Contract

*Culture and Cooperation
in Human Evolution*

KIM STERELNY

*Philosophy
RSSS Australian National University*

Oxford University Press is a department of the University of Oxford. It furthers
the University's objective of excellence in research, scholarship, and education
by publishing worldwide. Oxford is a registered trade mark of Oxford University
Press in the UK and certain other countries.

Published in the United States of America by Oxford University Press
198 Madison Avenue, New York, NY 10016, United States of America.

© Oxford University Press 2021

All rights reserved. No part of this publication may be reproduced, stored in
a retrieval system, or transmitted, in any form or by any means, without the
prior permission in writing of Oxford University Press, or as expressly permitted
by law, by license, or under terms agreed with the appropriate reproduction
rights organization. Inquiries concerning reproduction outside the scope of the
above should be sent to the Rights Department, Oxford University Press, at the
address above.

You must not circulate this work in any other form
and you must impose this same condition on any acquirer.

Library of Congress Control Number: 2020043282
ISBN 978-0-19-753138-9

DOI: 10.1093/oso/9780197531389.001.0001

For Midnight. And the other feline companions who have kept me such good company in my years in philosophy: Hegel, Satan, Scruff, Little Scruff, Artemis, Moss Bros, Diva, Pretta and Colette. Loved and missed.

Contents

Preface	ix
1. Building Cumulative Culture	1
1.1 Methodological Preliminaries	1
1.2 Culture and Cooperation	11
1.3 The Prehistory of an Unusual Ape	16
1.4 The Growing Footprint of Cultural Learning	26
1.5 Cumulative Cultural Learning	34
1.6 Adapted Minds and Environments	42
1.7 Overview	50
2. The Pleistocene Social Contract	54
2.1 Free-Riders and Bullies	54
2.2 Curbing Dominance Hierarchies	61
2.3 An Economy of Reciprocation	70
2.4 Making Reciprocation Work: Gossip	78
2.5 Making Reciprocation Work: Norms	82
2.6 Making Reciprocation Work: Ritual	88
2.7 Stabilizing Cooperation	92
3. Cooperation in a Larger World	93
3.1 Cooperation between Bands	93
3.2 The Origins of an Open Society	104
3.3 Cooperation, Culture and Conflict	111
3.4 Individual Selection, Group Selection and Cultural Group Selection	118
4. Cooperation in Hierarchical Communities	124
4.1 The Puzzle of Farming	124
4.2 Cooperation in an Unequal World	133

4.3 Religion, Ritual and Ideology 142
 4.4 Conflict, Hierarchy and Inequality 151

Epilogue: Why Only Us? 157

References 163
Index 179

Preface

Many books have a long prehistory, and this one is no exception. I began thinking about human social evolution around the turn of the century, largely in response to John Maynard Smith and Eors Szathmary, and their *Major Transitions in Evolution*. At that time, my core interest was in macroevolution and evolvability (the world has been spared my great work on that), and *Major Transitions* closes with the idea that the emergence of human social life was the final major transition (so far) in evolution. So my initial idea was to explore macroevolutionary issues and major transitions using hominin evolution as a stalking horse. Alas, the example ate the project, and for close to twenty years I have spent much of my time digging skeletons out of the hominin closet and with the direction of theoretical illumination going the other way. I used ideas about the importance of niche construction in evolutionary change; the importance of adaptive plasticity to evolutionary change, and ideas about the nature and role of non-genetic inheritance to illuminate the evolutionary trajectory through which we became such aberrant great apes. An initial sketch of these ideas was roughed out at the end of *Thought in a Hostile World*. That sketch, a view in which the downstream niche construction of the parental generation shaped the developmental environment of the incoming generation in ways that made further change possible, was fleshed out in *The Evolved Apprentice*. In turn, at the end, that book briefly engaged with the late Pleistocene transformation of hominin life. *The Pleistocene Social Contract* takes up that challenge more fully, while revisiting and (I hope) enriching the account of the earlier Pleistocene prequel to the complexities of late Pleistocene forager life.

So it has been a long trip to the Neolithic, and like most travellers, I have had a lot of help on the way. Early on, two of my postdocs, Ben Jeffares and Brett Calcott, were influential. Ben infected me with his scepticism about single case, big-breakthrough accounts of hominin evolution. Brett's work on cooperation shaped how I see the problem, with his clear separation between the explanation of the profits of cooperation, and an explanation of its stability. Much of the theoretical work, and virtually all of the work in experimental economics, has assumed that the benefits of cooperation are unproblematic. Rather, what needs explanation is why cooperation is stable (when it is) given the threat of defection. Brett (and after him, Jonathan Birch) showed that this is quite wrong: getting cooperation to work requires serious social and cognitive tools, whose existence requires explanation.

Over this whole period, my thinking has owed a lot to my regular interactions with Peter Godfrey-Smith, Russell Gray and Cecilia Heyes. Peter's specific influence has mostly come through his work on Darwinian populations, and his distinction between paradigm and marginal cases of such population. This has pushed me to be more sceptical of cultural group selection, and back toward a more individualist account of the hominin evolutionary trajectory. But he has also been my most regular and acute pre-publication critic, though more recently, Ron Planer has joined him in that role, with the added advantage of a very deep immersion in the same paleoanthropological literature that I mine. This book owes much to Ron. Russell has taught me always (I hope) to think phylogenetically and comparatively, and has perhaps slightly tempered my native adaptationism. He, like Celia Heyes, has also encouraged me to think more consistently about scenario testing as well as scenario construction. In addition to helping sensitize me to testability, Celia's own work is very challenging, in articulating a view in which genetically-based cognitive adaptations play very little role in hominin evolution. In more recent years, Peter Hiscock has come to influence my thinking a lot, especially through his deep scepticism about directional models of hominin evolutionary history. Despite his sceptical erosion, the overall picture of *The Pleistocene Social Contract* is directional. But it is I hope suitably sensitive to the illusions of directionality that can be easily generated by temporal biases in the material record. Finally, the last chapter of this book owes a lot to Trevor Watkins, who single-handedly hauled me out of the Palaeolithic and into the Neolithic and its challenges.

In this last twenty years I have been very fortunate in both my institutional and personal circumstances. Initially, I divided my time between the Victoria University of Wellington (New Zealand) and the Australian National University (ANU) (Canberra, Australia). Both were supportive, friendly, easy places at which to work, and with a regular flow of able and engaged students. In the last decade, I have been more or less exclusively at the ANU, a wonderful base, with terrific colleagues, further enriched by a great cohort of graduate students and a regular influx of visitors. I am also deeply indebted to the Australian Research Council for their regular and generous support of my research. This has enabled me to surround myself with terrific postdocs: Brett Calcott, Ben Fraser, Jess Isserow, Justin Bruner, Ron Planer, Anton Killin, Matt Spike. My personal situation has been equally conducive to pushing this project through to completion. As all my friends insist, I have been for many reasons fortunate in my choice of partner, Melanie Nolan. While most of those reasons are not for public consumption, one is. Melanie is much more committed to her research than am I, so there has never been a trace of disapproval as I disappeared off to my office or to a workshop. Likewise, our daughter Kate is tolerant of these eccentricities; indeed, she has dipped a toe into these academic waters herself.

Finally, I should specifically thank those who read and commented on this manuscript or its ancestors: Jonathan Birch, Carl Brusse, Chiara Ferrario, Peter Godfrey-Smith, Celia Heyes, Peter Hiscock, Tim Lewens, Ross Pain, Ron Planer, Kim Shaw-Williams and Joeri Witteveen.

The Pleistocene Social Contract

1
Building Cumulative Culture

1.1 Methodological Preliminaries

This book will present an account of the origins, elaboration and interaction of two very distinctive features of our lineage: our dependence on cooperation and our dependence on culture. In these respects, as in many others, we are very different from other primates. In my view, those differences emerged by positive feedback amongst a number of initially smaller divergences from the great ape stock. These include bipedal locomotion, improved causal and social reasoning, reproductive cooperation, increasing dependence on tools, changes in diet and foraging style. Interaction between these initially small departures from great ape lifeways drove an evolutionary trajectory that took us ever further from our great ape relatives. In contrast to many others, I do not see the distinctive features of human life as grounded in a key, difference-making innovation: not language, not understanding others; not a distinctive kind of cognitive flexibility (Mithen 1996, Deacon 1997, Tomasello 2014). I will begin with some methodological remarks, and some cautions about the empirical foundations of the analysis before ending this section with a brief sketch of my general framework.

The account is largely in the form of a narrative, and it begins in our deep past, shortly after the human lineage (collectively known as the hominins[1]) diverged from its sister lineage, the lineage whose living descendants are the two chimp species. The narrative is

---

[1] A note on terminology: I will use "hominin" for any member of this lineage. I will use "human" as an informal term for the late, large-brained members of this lineage.

developed as an explanation, not a mere chronicle: it is full of causal claims about the factors that drove the human evolutionary trajectory, and about their relative importance. However, as the narrative begins in the deep past, 6+ mya (mya = millions of years ago), it is reasonable to wonder whether any attempt to reconstruct the behaviours and ways of life of such long-extinct hominins is just baseless speculation. Indeed, there is a standard sneer that evolutionary narratives, especially human evolutionary narratives, are "just-so" stories: easy to produce, sometimes sounding plausible, and impossible to test (Gould and Lewontin 1978).

This suspicion is not entirely groundless. Traces of past lives disappear; the more distant in time those lives, the more those traces are lost. Those that remain must be interpreted through the lens of theory, and these are themselves controversial. Even so, the evolutionary narrative produced here is, I claim, detailed, coherent and empirically grounded. It identifies multiple, causally interconnected strands, linking foraging strategies, social structure, life history, reproductive strategies and intergenerational cultural learning.[2] What is said about each of these constrains what can be said about the others. Coherence, the mutual fit between these separate but causally interconnected elements, is a significant constraint on a complex evolutionary narrative, as any account of the rise of the hominins must be. Moreover, the narrative is empirically grounded at many points: if it is right, it predicts patterns in the traces left by our ancestors. For example, one causal hypothesis links a social change—increased social connection between residential groups—to a more reliable preservation of culturally transmitted information. If that hypothesis is right, signs of that social change should covary with signs of more reliable preservation and expansion of informational capital. In both cases, such traces will often

---

[2] A second note on terminology: some authors use "cultural learning" as a term for some advanced species of social learning. I use "cultural learning" and "social learning" as equivalents.

be faint or ambiguous. But they are not entirely missing. To recycle an analogy I have used elsewhere, in sending an agent under cover, an intelligence service has to construct a "legend": an innocent fake past of the agent. The construction of a legend becomes more difficult, as it becomes more complex and grounded. The more complex the legend, the more detail the agent has to remember, and the more difficult it is to retain coherence. Likewise, the more points at which the legend is vulnerable to external checks, the more difficult it is to construct. Contrary to the sneer, rich coherent narratives which make frequent contact with the data are not easy to construct. The narrative has gaps and is hostage to future discovery, but it is not a just-so story.[3]

In general, the empirical foundations of the explanatory framework developed here reflect consensus views in archaeology and palaeoanthropology. However, there are important exceptions to that claim. The picture of human evolution presented here, with its interaction between culture and cooperation, depends on three controversial claims about the past. The first is that our ancestors were competent, cooperative hunters in the distant past: probably as early as 1.8 mya. The second claim is not controversial as such; it is just not discussed. It is the idea that the character of human cooperation changed, between about 150 kya and 100 kya (kya = thousands of years ago) from cooperation as collective action to cooperation through reciprocation, through the exchange of aid. As I see it, these economic changes were initially much more marked in Africa; an economy of reciprocation developed later in the rest of the world. The third is that the threat of intergroup violence did not play a major role in structuring human social life until the Holocene, about 12 kya. I will explain my stance on these issues as they become relevant, but be warned.

---

[3] For a more extensive version of this argument, see (Currie and Sterelny 2017); for an extended defence of the historical sciences, see (Currie 2018).

While the narrative presented here is not a mere speculation, there is no denying that there are important gaps in the historical record. That is especially true of the earlier hominins. Even so, the empirical record is somewhat richer than one might suppose. For example, there is a much richer fossil record of human evolution than there is of chimp evolution, and that itself tells us something important about the different distributions and habitats of the two lineages. Hominin fossils tell us a good deal about hominin lifeways: about their diet; about their physical capacities (for example, the hands, feet and shoulders of obligately bipedal hominins differ from those hominins who still spent a good deal of time in trees); about their habitat preferences (if fossils are found where the hominin died); about their success in dispersing over landmasses; about their life history (teeth sometimes indicate age at sexual maturity). Isotope data can tell us something about diet and even movement patterns (Lugli, Cipriani et al. 2019). Fossils even sometimes hint at social organization (for example, when fossils show evidence of surviving injury or illness that would have required care from others;[4] conversely, evidence of violent death). In addition to the fossils themselves, from a bit earlier than 3 mya, we begin to have evidence of their material culture, and of the uses of that culture. That is most directly from the debris they left behind them (their middens, camp sites, work sites), but also from tools with their wear patterns. Unfortunately, this evidence is limited in three important ways. First, unless by amazing fluke, we will find evidence only of common products and activities, and the deeper in time, the more we see only the commonest phenomena. Second, sites disappear or degrade over time, but not equally. There are biases: from example, many Pleistocene sea-edge sites are now under water. Third, with rare exceptions, we see only hard material

---

[4] There is evidence of care as far back as around 1.5 mya, from an individual whose diseases would have left him unable to forage or defend himself (Spikins, Rutherford et al. 2010).

technology and hard detritus. That said, stone technology is both especially revealing and important. Working stone is unforgiving and dangerous, as striking stone can send sharp flakes flying off in unpredictable directions. But it also gives the stone worker access to other materials. Wood, hide and fibre can be worked with stone, whereas soft materials cannot be used to transform other soft materials. Lithics are a keystone technology.

Three-million-year-old rubbish dumps do tell us about three-million-years-gone lives, but only with the help of theories and models which tell us what the traces from the past are traces of (Currie 2018). Some of these theories are very specific: for example, about the chemical and physical differences between domestic and wild fires. Others are much more general: about the economics of foraging, or the costs and benefits of different ways of managing risk. The role of theories and models in interpreting traces expands our evidential base: current (and near-past) observations become relevant, because those theories must themselves be tested and calibrated. Some of these observations are from experiments: what can a certain kind of stone tool cut, and what does the edge look like afterwards? What does a bone look like after it is first butchered and then gnawed by hyenas, rather than vice versa? Can a thrown wooden, untipped spear penetrate zebra hide, and from what distance (Churchill 1993, Churchill and Rhodes 2009, Salem and Churchill 2016)? But others are from observations of ethnographically known foragers and other small scale societies. That is not because (say) the San of Southern Africa or the Hadza of East Africa are living fossils of Pleistocene lifeways. Rather, as Frank Marlowe says in discussing the Hadza (Marlowe 2010), it is because information about such peoples tests and calibrates our general models of forager economics and forager ecology. In building these general models, the diversity of forager experience is important. Robert Kelly's superb survey emphasizes that diversity (Kelly 2013), and it is critical in showing the response of forager economic and social organisation to environmental variation. In turn, those general models guide our interpretation of the traces they have left. For example, we know from ethnography that in many environments most hunts fail, even for the most skilled hunters. In those environments, gathered resources were critical, probably implying some form of division of labour. Likewise, we can estimate the size range of ancient forager bands from the ecological economics of ethnographically known bands (Kelly 2013). We cannot automatically assume that the forager economies of the Pliocene and Pleistocene were like those of the recent past. But if we do think they were different, we need to identify a factor (or factors) that makes them different.

In short: the attempt to understand the lifeways of our ancestors and the ways those lifeways served as foundation and springboard to ours is challenging. But it is not hopeless.

This essay builds on my previous work on the evolution of human social life, and on the cognitive capacities that support that life (or those lives). In particular, it relies upon a view of human cognition that emphasizes its plasticity. We have the capacity to acquire new skills for which we do not have specific genetic preparation, and we can re-purpose existing cognitive circuits to new tasks. This adaptive plasticity allowed our ancestors to acquire novel capacities, and sometimes these were important enough to reshape ancestral niches; stone tool making and fire control were probably examples of niche-changing new skills. Once lifeways change, so too do the selective forces acting on those hominins, ultimately changing their genetic makeup. This process has iterated through hominin evolution. So while I agree that gene-culture co-evolution has built human biology, and in ways relevant to human cognition, change typically began with behavioural innovations that were expressions of our adaptive plasticity. In West-Eberhart's phrasing, genes are the followers, not the leaders, of phenotypic change. While not yet orthodoxy, this view is no longer heterodox. See, for example, (Heyes 2018), (Anderson 2014). On the basis of this assumption about hominin plasticity, I develop two novel claims: one about cooperation; the other about culture, and their coevolution.

The book itself is organized around a distinctive four-phase model of the emergence of the extraordinary forms of cooperation on which contemporary life depends. I take the first phase to be the suppression of the dominance hierarchy that early hominins would have inherited in some form as the great ape pattern. This suppression allowed a form of foraging that depended on collective action to stabilize and expand. Here the argument partially converges with that of Michael Tomasello, who also argues that collective action with immediate returns played a foundational role in hominin evolution (Tomasello, Melis et al. 2012, Tomasello 2016). The next phase is the transition from a foraging economy based on immediate return mutualism to one in which direct and indirect reciprocation was increasingly important. While still very profitable, the stability of this form of cooperation depended on new cultural and cognitive tools. The third phase is an expansion of the social and spatial scale of cooperation, as residential groups became networked with one another forming larger communities, although the second and third phase are separated more analytically than temporally. However, as chapter 3 shows, an expansion of the social and spatial scale of cooperation (or even passive tolerance of those outside the immediate circle of daily interaction) poses novel problems. That is especially true if the ancestral atom of hominin social organization even roughly resembled the chimp residential group, with its extreme unease with outsiders. Human residential groups are open rather than closed, and as hominin residential groups gradually became connected in larger networks, those networks made it possible, in some cases at least, to solve cooperation and collective action problems at larger scales than the forager band. There are many uncertainties about the baseline and timing of this transition, but in chapter 3 I offer an incremental account of this transformation. Neither the second nor the third phase have been the focus of much attention. In contrast, there has been much attention on the fourth transition, the (re-)-establishment of hierarchical societies, and the continued (even expanded) role of cooperation despite inequality. This attention is no surprize, for as well shall see in 2.1, the coexistence of serious inequality and continued cooperation is puzzling. I offer my own account, drawing on ideas from Ray Kelly, Robert Kelly and Brian Haydon,[5] but differing from them in important ways too. The account I offer places considerable weight on the prior evolution of a hierarchy of esteem, and with it, the oblique intergenerational transmission of the norms and mores of a community. Moreover, I also emphasize the limited opportunities of collective action from below, and give an account of why those opportunities are so limited.

This analysis of the growth and transformation of cooperation is tied to an account of culture and cultural evolution. This account builds on the analysis of *The Evolved Apprentice* (Sterelny 2012). I am part of the almost universal consensus in agreeing that in our lineage, cultural learning has become cumulative, and that is a critical difference between late hominins and almost all the cultural learning of almost all other animals. I also accept the consensus that one form of cumulative culture, incremental improvement of an existing capacity, depends on the high fidelity transmission of information across the generations. However, I depart from that consensus in two, linked ways. I do not think high fidelity cultural learning depends on a specific cognitive adaptation, and I think its importance to cumulative culture has been over-stated. So, first, I doubt that cumulative culture depends on a specific cognitive adaptation, a cognitive breakthrough that made cumulative culture possible. For in my view, high fidelity transmission across the generations does *not* depend on high fidelity individual learning episodes. Consider, for example, a sub-adult learning to make an adhesive, one which can only be made through a precisely ordered sequence, and then learning to use that adhesive to attach a

---

[5] See (Kelly 2000, Kelly 2013, Hayden 2014, Hayden 2018).

point to a shaft. That juvenile is likely to have many opportunities to watch expert performance and demonstration, and to eavesdrop on peers. For in forager life, much takes place in the open in public view (Hewlett, Hudson et al. 2019). The sub-adult is likely to have many opportunities to experiment, supplementing socially sourced information with trial and error. Even if there is a lot of noise in the flow of information in a specific learning episode, intergenerational transmission can be high fidelity, if the incoming generation has the capacity to detect their own errors (from signals from the world, or from their elders), and the motivation and the support to locate and correct them. So one important claim is that *there are many roads to high fidelity*. That being so, it follows that cumulative culture via incremental improvement does not depend on the prior evolution of some specific cognitive adaptation for cultural learning. I do not think accurate imitation learning and/or collective intentionality are essential prerequisites for accumulating cultural knowledge across a series of generations. Very likely, as cultural learning became increasingly central to hominin lives, gene-culture coevolution tuned human minds to those new demands. We became better at cultural learning. Even so, culture and cumulative culture became important in our lineage before those cognitive changes, whatever they might be.

Second, the importance of high fidelity transmission to cumulative culture has been over-stated; it is essential for only one form of cumulative culture. For cumulative culture has often been described by analogy with the genetic evolution of complex adaptation, and is hence seen only as the incremental improvement of existing capacities (Tomasello 1999, Tennie, Braun et al. 2016, Tennie, Premo et al. 2017, Tennie, Hopper et al. forthcoming). This is too narrow a characterization, and one that has led to an excessive focus on imitation as the critical cognitive capacity on which cumulative culture rests. Indeed, despite their focus on imitation, Michael Tomasello and Claudio Tennie have introduced a vivid metaphor for an alternative and much broader conception of cumulative cultural evolution, through their idea of a "zone of latent solutions (ZLS)".

An ability is within this zone, if an agent could acquire it fairly readily by individual learning, even if de facto it is learned socially. For Pleistocene hominins, the location of nearby waterholes was surely within their zone, if even most learned those locations as juveniles accompanying their mother. Obviously, an ability that could *only* be learned socially is outside the zone. So we can think of the difference between ordinary cultural learning and cumulative cultural learning, as this: cumulative cultural learning enables agents to gain capacities that clearly lie outside their ZLS, whereas ordinary cultural learning, of the kind widespread across animal lineages, only enables those animals to find solutions within that zone, though perhaps more quickly or with less risk. Importantly, the concepts of cumulative culture as (i) building capacities by incremental improvement, and (ii) enabling agents to acquire capacities outside their ZLS are not equivalent. While most abilities/technologies that are the result of incremental improvement are probably outside an agent's ZLS, the converse is not true. We have many capacities that we can acquire only through the greater efficiency of cultural learning. This is most importantly exemplified in forager's famously extensive natural history knowledge of their patch. Very likely, any single item in their information store could be individually learned, but not the whole of it. Likewise, cultural learning enables agents to combine and cross-fertilize information streams from different domains (Muthukrishna and Henrich 2016): in finding out about the world, the division of labour is a powerful tool. Cumulative cultural learning combines (i) increases in the bandwidth of learning, (ii) incremental improvement and (iii) novel recombination, and this is another reason to reject the idea that cumulative cultural learning is grounded in some single, specific cognitive adaptation.

In the rest of this book, I sketch a dynamic in which the expansion of cultural learning, including cumulative cultural learning in this broader sense, in our lineage supports the expansion and transformation of cooperation in our lineage. Moreover, these new forms of cooperation, in turn, make cultural learning more powerful, more pervasive in its effects on hominin lifeways. Culture and cooperation evolve together.

In very brief summary then, the argument of this book will depend (i) on the idea that large game hunting was important early in our evolutionary career, but that inter-group violence became a serious threat only late in that career; (ii) on a four-stage model of the emergence of our distinctive form of cooperation, and (iii) on the claim that cultural learning, including cumulative cultural learning, became important early, but without depending on special purpose cognitive adaptations. OK. You have been warned about what lies ahead, and what is new and controversial. Let's go.

1.2 Culture and Cooperation

When agents act together, there are often synergies. Their collective output is greater than the sum of their individual outputs, were they to act as lone wolves. In such circumstances, there is a cooperation dividend. That dividend can be the result of collective action: a group of musk oxen standing together, acting in concert, can see off a wolf pack attack that would be extremely dangerous to any individual ox; a group of wolves can kill an ox that would be fairly safe against any individual wolf. It can be the result of complementarity and the division of labour. Eusocial insect colonies exemplify the power of collective action, but there is also a good deal of pooled individual action, mediated by the division of labour and caste differentiation. In many forager societies, the sexual division of labour is collectively profitable, as it enables the different sexes to specialize on different targets in different places, with appropriate tools and skills (O'Connell 2006). If both sexes targeted the same resources, they would deplete more rapidly, and other resources would go untouched. Cooperation can manage risk, by protecting against unpredictable fluctuations in the environment. If we allow your people to forage in our territory in your drought years, in return for our right to forage in yours in our droughts, we are both buffered against environmental risk. If you share with me when I am sick or injured, and I share with you when you have a similar misfortune, we are both protected. An explanation of any particular form of cooperation has to show why it is profitable, and how that form of cooperation could emerge incrementally from a noncooperative or less cooperative predecessor. This is the *generation-of-benefit* problem.

An explanation of cooperation also has to explain why cooperation is stable. Notoriously, in many cooperative interactions, while all co-operators are better off if they all cooperate than they would be if none of them cooperate, each agent is better off if he/she does not cooperate, and everyone else does. For acting cooperatively often has costs: risk, energy, opportunity costs. Yet the profit of the cooperative interaction often does not require that every agent that stands to gain also needs to pay their full share of those costs. Indeed, in collective actions, the profitable outcome is more robust if there is some redundancy; if not every wolf has to be at the right place at the right moment. Otherwise collection action is profitable only if coordination is perfect (Birch 2012). This creates the famous evolutionary temptation to defect or free-ride; to accept help when I am injured, and then stint on helping others. This is the *distribution-of-benefit* problem (this way of framing the issues is from (Calcott 2008)). Once agents begin to cheat, others do too, and cooperation erodes. Benefit must be distributed in ways that incentivize further cooperation. These acidic effects of uncontrolled free-riding on cooperation make contemporary societies deeply puzzling. Almost all of us live in large scale social worlds where we depend on cooperation for virtually every necessity of life (Seabright 2010). Yet these are also highly unequal worlds in which tiny elites skim off a huge slice of the social surplus. Paradoxically, contemporary society seems to combine extensive cooperation with rampant freeriding; a puzzle to which we return in 4.2–4.4.

Despite spectacular cooperation failures, contemporary humans have clearly solved both problems, though almost always in partial and error-prone ways. In comparison to most mammals and most primates, we are spectacularly cooperative. This is true of the deep history of our lineage; we have been obligate co-operators for hundreds of thousands of years; perhaps millions of years. This book is about the role of hominin culture in the solution of both the generation and the distribution problem. We have become more culture-dependent as our cooperation has become more pervasive, and as the imprint of culture has increased, we have become more cooperative. Hominins are both extremely cooperative primates and encultured primates.

Contemporary humans are encultured in a very rich sense. Our sense of our own identity is complexly entangled with the history, the mores, the legends and the collective experience of the social groups in which we are embedded. We do not just live in specific communities, we consciously identify with the communities of which we are a part, and advertise that identification in dress, accent and other insignias. I do not deny the importance of that rich sense of culture,[6] but here I will mostly be writing of culture in a more mundane sense. What we know, what we believe, what we can do and even to a considerable extent what we want, is learned from other hominins. Over the approximately seven million years of hominin history,[7] cultural learning has had an increasing imprint

---

[6] This rich sense of culture is often linked to a further claim: a conception of a community's culture as a cohesive, integrated system. The extent to which the elements of a culture are linked is an empirical question, but I am persuaded by Sperber's arguments that the more extreme versions of holistic views are untenable, as they have no adequate account of either variation within the one community, nor of the fact that cultures can change piecemeal (Sperber 1996). This becomes relevant again in 4.4.

[7] There is actually a good deal of variation in molecular clock estimates of the divergence of the human and chimp lineages; some are as deep as 12 mya; some as recent as 5 mya. For a brief introduction to these complexities, see (Jensen-Seaman and Hooper-Boyd 2013). For a more extensive but exceptionally clear introduction to the use of molecular methods to estimate the dates of evolutionary divergences, see Bromham,

on hominin minds. In that sense, we have become increasingly encultured.

When the more expert aid the less expert, cultural learning is information sharing, and sharing information, like sharing any other resource, is a form of cooperation. Early in hominin evolution, much social learning was probably just a by-product of adult activities: informed action in the world created public information, and the less informed took advantage of that information. A juvenile with her mother will have many opportunities to see what her mother identifies as food, what she takes to be dangerous, who she identifies as an ally and so on. One major change in the hominin lineage took place as the informed began to actively facilitate this uptake, sharing what they know; perhaps a little under 2 mya (Hiscock 2014). On this picture, the growth of cultural learning in our lineage is both the expansion of a form of cooperation and an amplifier of cooperation. Shared information and shared technique, over deep time, has made collective action and other forms of more directly material cooperation more powerful, and it has also provided tools that help control the threat of free-riding. These material benefits of information sharing, once established, came to select for the cognitive capacities and social interactions that made cultural learning more reliable.

I have claimed that hominins diverged from other great apes via positive feedback loops between initially much smaller differences. One of those loops was between information-sharing and other forms of cooperation. An expansion of one is apt to open up space for the other. Thus reproductive cooperation, an important and perhaps early evolving element of hominin reproductive strategies, opens up more space for social learning by very young infants, by exposing them to more sources of information (Burkart, Hrdy et al. 2009). Bipedalism increases the benefits of reproductive

---

L. (2016). *An Introduction to Molecular Evolution and Phylogenetics*. Oxford, Oxford University Press, chapters 13 and 14.

cooperation, for once hominins walked upright, their infants could no longer ride safely and conveniently on their backs. Some form of creching would be very beneficial (especially, of course, as hominin infants became ever more immature at birth).[8] The same is true of cooperation in the acquisition of resources. Perhaps sometime in the late Pliocene, near Pliocene/Pleistocene boundary, hominins gradually evolved a new lifeway centred on collaborative foragers targeting high value resources (Thompson, Carvalho et al. 2019). These resources are typically hard to find, heavily defended, or both. Animals defend aggressively; have vigorous and well-honed escape routines; hide, are camouflaged; rest in inaccessible places. Plants defend themselves mechanically (with thorns and shells) and chemically. Harvesting such resources depends on a blend of cooperation, technology and expertise.

To pick just one example, in seasonal, subtropical areas many plants survive the dry by growing underground storage organs (tubers, corms, collectively, "USO"s). These are potentially rich sources of energy, full of carbohydrates (Laden and Wrangham 2005, Wrangham, Cheney et al. 2009). To harvest them, foragers have to recognize the right plant, which is not easy, since in the dry many of these plants are unobtrusive, nondescript stalks. They have to be dug out, which requires a robust, sharp digging stick. Once extracted, many USOs require processing to be made edible. In the right environments, they are available in quantity. But they are demanding targets. Even more obviously, the same is true of meat, brains and marrow from medium and large game. Harvesting game, either by direct hunting or by pirating the kills of other predators, requires a weapons technology, rich information about the habitat and the habits of the target animal, and, at least until the relatively recent invention of projectile technology, cooperation between the foragers. Yet efficient harvesting of resources, together

---

[8] Here is just one place where our ignorance of soft material technology is troubling: we have no idea when baby slings were invented.

with an effective collective response to predators, makes a slower life history possible, giving juveniles more time to acquire skills and information, and adults more time to hone their skills and add to their information store through experience (Kaplan, Hooper et al. 2009). There is positive feedback between the efficient capture of difficult but rich resources, cultural learning and a slow life history. Adult profit supports juvenile skill acquisition, in turn making their future activities as adults profitable.

This general picture is not controversial. There are vigorous debates on detail: for example, the role and relative importance of hunting vs gathering and scavenging; the relative importance of size and skill; the cognitive prerequisites of cultural learning. There are debates about exactly when cultural learning became essential (Corbey, Jagich et al. 2016, Tennie, Braun et al. 2016), linked to debates about when hominins became dependent on stone tools (Shea 2017). But few would disagree that by the mid-Pleistocene, hominins depended on some combination of technology, cooperation and expertise. These all depend in various ways on cultural learning. This chapter is mostly about how and why cultural learning came to have such a massive footprint in our history, and on the effect of cultural learning in amplifying the benefits of cooperation. The next chapter is focussed on distribution; on the control of freeriding and the increasing difficulty of that control through the second transition. To put these projects into context, what follows is a brief overview of hominin history.

1.3 The Prehistory of an Unusual Ape

Identifiable hominin fossils date back into the Miocene and through the Pliocene, but the main morphological changes that make us look very different from other great apes—bipedalism and encephalization—seem to have mostly taken place from the end of the Pliocene and through the Pleistocene (Table 1.1).

Table 1.1 Navigating the Epochs

Epoch	Dates before Present
Miocene	23.03–5.3 mya
Pliocene	5.33–2.58 mya
Pleistocene	2.58 mya–11,700 ya
Holocene	11,700 ya–present

Before giving a thumbnail sketch of hominin history from our divergence from the chimp lineage (probably at about 7 mya), a couple of initial cautions are in order. Much is not known. Especially for the first 4 million years of this period, fossils are few, and many are fragmentary. Only at the very end is there archaeological material: that is, evidence from the products of hominin action (tools, middens and the like), and even that is controversial. So all of what follows remains somewhat conjectural; some is very conjectural. Second, in the technical paleoanthropological literature there is a lot of debate about taxonomy: about assigning fossils to specific species, and, often, defending claims about species identity and difference. I do not place much weight on specific species identification in the Miocene, Pliocene and much of the Pleistocene: fossils are often fragmentary, and they are typically so rare that we have little evidence of the natural variation within these species. So when I use specific species names like *habilus*, *erectus* and *Heidelbergensis*, I use these to indicate a shift in morphology and probably behaviour over time. These are successively larger and more encephalized hominins (that is, the ratio of brain size to body size has increased). They are successively somewhat more similar to very recent humans. But we do not know how many biological species of hominins there were, say, a million years ago: we do not know whether there were reproductively isolated but morphologically similar lineages existing at the same time. Moreover, evidence of some gene flow between Anatomically Modern Humans

(AMHs), Denisovans and Neanderthals suggests that there can be gene flow between morphologically distinguishable lineages.

One obvious and notorious difference between humans and other great apes is our relatively and absolutely large brain. There are uncertainties about the history of hominin brain expansion, but Table 1.2 offers a rough guide.

This table illustrates a general trend, but it should be read with a lot of caution. For one thing, body size also matters: as bodies get larger, brains get larger too. For another, in some cases, especially with *erectus*, there is a large variation both regionally but also temporally, with later erectines typically larger-brained: see (Klein 2009) pp 306–307. Finally, it can be argued that neural density is critical, and this is not constant over mammals or even primates: see (Herculano-Houzel 2016). That said, the earliest hominins (ardipithicenes and australopithecines) had approximately chimp-sized brains; they seemed to live in somewhat more open and seasonal habitats than the *pan* species. At least some were habitually bipedal, but it is less clear when they become obligately bipedal. Some of these early hominins seem to have retained

Table 1.2 Hominin Brains over Time

Species	Brain Volume in cubic centimetres	Reference
Australopithecines	434–530	(Klein 2009) p 198
Homo habilis	Approx. 650	(Gamble, Dunbar et al. 2014) p 99
Homo erectus	Average 950	(Rightmire 2013)
Homo Heidelbergensis	Average 1230 cc	(Klein 2009, Rightmire 2013) (Rightmire 2013)
Upper Palaeolithic Sapiens	Average 1577 (+/- 135	(Klein 2009) p 308
European and West Asian Classic Neanderthals	Average 1435 (+/- 184)	(Klein 2009) p 309

adaptations for climbing, so they may have continued to nest in trees, and hence remained tied to wooded areas for safer resting places at night. Australopithecines were significantly smaller than later hominins. As such, they would have been vulnerable to the impressive Pliocene and Pleistocene African predators. Towards the end of the Pliocene, this lineage seemed to split into a robust branch (adapted to eat tough vegetable foods requiring powerful jaws and teeth) and a gracile lineage. On the standard story, our direct ancestors come from the gracile australopithecines. Late australopithecines are thought to be the first to make and use stone tools. The first somewhat controversial examples are dated at about 3.4 mya (McPherron, Alemseged et al. 2010, Harmand, Lewis et al. 2015). Uncontroversial Oldowan tools—cores with sharp flakes struck off, and with animal bones that show evidence of their use—date from 2.5 mya (Braun, Aldeias et al. 2019). These were probably made and used by a transitional species, *habilus*, once recognized as the first member of the Homo genus, now often demoted to the australopithecines. So far, this history looks like business as usual: a lineage of great apes diversifying through local adaptation to more seasonal and more open habitats. That changes in the Pleistocene.

There is some controversy about whether encephalization was under way with the habilines. It is uncontroversially underway with hominins appearing a little under 2 mya, *Homo Erectus*[9] (Shultz, Nelson et al. 2012). Erectines were considerably bigger than early hominins (though the largest erectines were still a good deal smaller than the largest recent hominins); they were significantly encephalized, and there is evidence that their life history was more like that of modern hominins, with a longer lifespan, and longer periods of juvenile dependence. The crucial point is that the erectines took off: within 200 k years, they had spread through Africa, through much of Eurasia to China and deep into South East

---

[9] There are other named species through this period as well, most often *Homo ergaster*.

Asia, as they were in Java 1.9 mya (Finlayson 2014). Perhaps they arrived somewhat later in West Europe. The early erectines provide the first good evidence of hunting large and medium size game (Bunn and Pickering 2010, Pickering and Bunn 2012, Pickering 2013, Domínguez-Rodrigo and Pickering 2017). In addition, at least some erectine groups seem to be responsible for important technical innovations, as one might expect, given their larger brains.

One of these might be fire. Fire is difficult to detect in the physical record. There is a scatter of plausible erectine sites perhaps with domestic fire in Africa earlier than 1 mya (Gowlett and Wrangham 2013, Gowlett 2016, Wrangham 2017), but there are no undeniable sites of domestic fire until about 800 kya, and even those hominins may not have been able to ignite fire at will. Almost certainly, fire was domesticated in stages, perhaps with losses as well as gains, and with the exploitation and management of natural fire long preceding ignition control. But the evidence suggests that this trajectory began with some erectines. More certainly, erectines were the first to use an impressive new technology, Acheulian stone-working techniques. The signature product is the famous tear-drop shaped symmetrical handaxe. These artefacts were much more technically demanding than Oldowan cobble and flake technology, though as with fire, many erectine sites are without Acheulian remains, as the technology seems to have been confined to, or near, Africa before 1 mya. The new technology, the rapid expansion out of Africa, the evidence of hunting and perhaps the first stages of fire domestication, suggest the beginnings of a shift to a new evolutionary dynamic with both cultural learning and cooperation playing a more important role.

Erectus-like hominins lived through most of the Pleistocene, with fossils found in Java to 100 kya (and even more recently, if *Homo floresiensis*[10] was a shrunken erectine). But at around 800 kya, it

---

[10] Floresiensis was the very small and surprisingly recent hominin whose fossils and artefacts have been found on Flores, in Indonesia.

was replaced in Africa and Europe (and perhaps Eurasia) by *Homo Heidelbergensis*. This species is the presumptive common ancestor to AMHs, Neanderthals and Denisovans. The Heidelbergensians were further encephalized, with their brain size range overlapping those of recent hominins. From the neck down, they were very similar to those recent hominins, as were the erectines. As far as we can tell, Heidelbergensian lives were more efficient versions of erectine lives. Claims about early erectine hunting remain somewhat controversial, but there is no doubt that Heidelbergensians were successful large game hunters (Jones 2007, Stiner 2013). Indeed, their hunting was reliable enough for them to colonize cool temperate habitats (Mussi 2007). These have few plant-based foods available over winter. For foragers in cool temperate climates, hunting must do more than provide an occasional and welcome supplement to a plant-based economy. That may have been the role of hunting in the erectine economy. Heidelbergensian use of fire is much more certain, though there is a large gap in the fire record between 780 kya and 400 kya. So it is still not clear whether and when they controlled ignition. For much of the life of the species, Heidelbergensians continued to depend on Acheulian techniques. However, around the time they faded into AMHs and Neanderthals, about 300 kya, so-called Middle Stone Age (MSA) techniques become more common,[11] techniques which gave knappers greater control over form. Similarly, from about 500 kya, we begin to get hints of hafting, of multi-component stone tools (Wilkins and Chazan 2012, Wilkins, Schoville et al. 2012).

These dates are not immutable. There has been a general trend, as research has continued, for the first appearance dates of signature technologies to shift deeper in time. This includes evidence of hafting, especially of microliths, small sharp shaped stone flakes (often with quite regular forms) that probably served as points or

---

[11] So far, nothing is known of Denisovan technology or their economy; they speak to us only through their DNA.

barbs on shafts. It includes evidence of "Levallois" stone working techniques. These are demanding techniques that give artisans greater control over form. This is the distinctive technology of the MSA, but there are hints of earlier appearances. There are possible indications of hafting as early as 780 kya, and more reliable signs of hafting and MSA techniques from about 500 kya (Kuhn 2020), but these tools were not yet typical of archaeological materials. Composite tools and Levallois techniques established and spread slowly, probably with losses as well as gains, and perhaps in part by independent discovery in different regions. The period after 300kya was the time at which hafting and Levallois shaping became well established and widespread, not the time of first discovery.

This distinction between origin and widespread use is particularly important in considering the next phase of hominin technical evolution, the Upper Palaeolithic. For through the 1980s and 1990s, it was believed that the MSA ended abruptly, about 50 kya, with the Upper Palaeolithic Revolution. The thought was that that revolution ushered in a more diverse and regionally varied stone technology; the more systematic use of bone, ivory and other durable materials (including awls and needles, indicators of fitted clothes); the exploitation of a broader range of resources, especially marine and riverine resources; and perhaps most striking of all, the production and use of material symbols. There was evidence of jewellery; ochre use; tools made in different styles, apparently independently of utilitarian considerations; the first music instruments (bone flutes at about 45 kya); mortuary rituals. It is now known that this supposed signal of a much richer, much more regionally varied, and much less obviously utilitarian lifeway was an artefact of a misleading European record (McBrearty and Brooks 2000, McBrearty 2007). The African record from about 250 kya on includes microliths supposedly a signature of the Upper Palaeolithic, though these are initially sporadic and widely spaced. Likewise, from about the same time, there is evidence of ochre, grindstones and other evidence of a broader resource base. There are burials from a little before 100 kya (Pettitt 2011, Pettitt 2015). The first known examples of jewellery and incised ochre are dated to between 100 kya and 80 kya (Rossano 2015), and through this period there is no doubt that these hominins had full control of fire. There was no abrupt, revolutionary change at about 50 kya. Instead, from about 250 kya, and especially after about 120 kya, the pace of change and regional differentiation accelerated, and material symbolism became visible in the archaeological record (Kuhn 2020). Even so, many gaps and reversions interrupted and complicated this general trend.[12]

Summing up this sprint through hominin history, three features stand out. (i) Morphological and behavioural divergence from the great apes has been rapid and spectacular, (ii) but the pace of divergence has not been even and (iii) morphological and behavioural changes do not seem well correlated. Taking these in sequence, first, by the normal standards of mammalian evolution, the extent to which hominins differed from other great apes, and the rate of that differentiation, was indeed remarkable, especially through the Pleistocene. At the beginning of the Pleistocene, the hominins were still an East African lineage (as far as we know, but see (Zhu, Dennell et al. 2018)). Perhaps they were just beginning to depend on technology, cooperation, meat and hunting in ways that marked them off from other great apes. They were becoming morphologically less like other great apes through their full commitment to bipedal existence, releasing arms, shoulders, wrists and hands from the constraints imposed by a role in locomotion. By the beginning of the Holocene, our species was very different from any other great ape. We were tall, gracile, encephalized and fragile by comparison to chimps and other great apes. We had diverse and regionally appropriate technology, and a cosmopolitan distribution.[13]

---

[12] So too are the complications caused by a general problem of interpretation: as we get closer to the present, we find more stuff, because a higher proportion of sites have survived.

[13] Far exceeding the grey wolf, the next most widely distributed large mammal, originally found through most of Eurasia and North America, but not Africa, Australia, Island South East Asia or South America.

Human ecological impacts at and before the Holocene were by no means negligible (they may have been responsible for an extinction wave in America). While estimating ancient population sizes is exceedingly error prone, even at low population densities, the enormous late Pleistocene/early Holocene distribution implies a very significant total population. Human social lives at the dawn of the Holocene were already very complex with multiple layers of vertical organization, as bands were connected to others through kinship, exchange, shared language and culture. Social life was influenced by language, explicit norms, religious traditions, kinship networks (often very elaborate ones), explicit ethnic identities. While these aspects of social structure are difficult to identify archaeologically, they are such an entrenched and cosmopolitan feature of forager life, it is very likely that they established in AMH social worlds before the out-of-Africa expansion, perhaps 80 kya. The speed and scale of this transformation calls for some form of special explanation.

Second, while it is true that hominins have ended up very different from other great apes in their morphology, social lives, ecology and technology, the rate of change has not been even. That is especially and most obviously true of technology, or at least hard material technology. At first change was very slow: Lomekwian tools from about 3.3 mya; Oldowan technology from about 2.5 mya, then joined by Acheulian technology (though not everywhere) from about 1.8 mya. Fire was very slowly domesticated. Only from about 250 kya do technological innovations take less than 100 millennia to establish. So if there has been a feedback loop linking ecological cooperation, technology and social learning, for a very long time that loop was fragile and easily stalled. While the divergence between the *pan* and the *hominin* lineage is now extremely striking, that divergence was not the result of a smoothly increasing trend. Rather, for millions of years it operated in spurts and long stalls.

Third, to the extent that we can identify the appearance of new hominin species in the record, there is strikingly little correlation between technical innovation and hominin speciation. With the very partial exception of the link between erectus and the Acheulian,[14] the arrival of a new hominin species was not the arrival of new technology. Even that exception is very partial. Acheulian tools are only found away from Africa from about 800 kya, long after the initial erectine expansion (Kuhn 2020). Moreover, Clive Finlayson notes that there are no Acheulian tools at a couple of the early African erectus sites (Finlayson 2014). Likewise, there is little obvious correlation between technical and behavioural change with encephalization, again with only the erectines as very partial exceptions. There was significant encephalization between 1.7 mya and the origins of the Heidelbergensians, at about 800 kya, without marked changes in hominin technology. Likewise, the last 100 k years has seen remarkable innovation without appreciable encephalization. So an explanation of the hominin pattern needs to explain both the late hominin acceleration of change and the independence of technical change, speciation pattern and encephalization. As we shall shortly see, one factor that helps explain this lack of correlation is cultural learning. The social environment, not just intrinsic neural equipment, increasingly shaped the technical and behavioural capacities of hominins.

The aim of the next section is to link this very broad-brush overview to the expansion of cultural learning. For it is that expansion that provided hominins with the physical tools, information and expertise that made cooperation increasingly profitable.

---

[14] It has standardly been argued that the Acheulian handaxe is found in Europe, India and Africa, but not east of the Movius Line, hence not in East Asia or South East Asia, but this turns on controversial claims about how to classify artefacts from those eastern areas.

1.4 The Growing Footprint of Cultural Learning

Humans now have extensive genetic and cultural adaptations that support high bandwidth, high fidelity, cultural learning. While there is broad consensus on this, there is very considerable debate about the character of these adaptations. One version of evolutionary psychology, made popular by Stephen Pinker, supposes that the adapted mind consists of a set of genetically pre-wired special purpose cognitive modules, each of which pre-adapts our learning to particular tasks and environments (Barkow, Cosmides et al. 1992, Sperber 1996, Pinker 1997, Mercier and Sperber 2017). While Michael Tomasello has a different view of the adaptations on which human culture depends, he too thinks we are genetically adapted to learn culturally and to act in concert with one another (Tomasello 2014, Tomasello 2016). In sharp contrast, Celia Heyes has argued that while our attention and motivations are genetically tuned, our cognitive specializations for culture (like language and theory of mind) were built culturally (Heyes 2018). I outlined my own views at the end of 1.1, and these are rather closer to Heyes, but include a much greater role for gene/culture coevolution in building these cognitive specializations. Moreover, I emphasize the importance of learning environments that are adaptively structured to support the acquisition of crucial competences (Sterelny 2003, Sterelny 2012). So while I suspect that contemporary human minds are genetically adapted for cultural learning, there is selection for genetic adaptations for such learning only in environments in which cultural learning is already important. So an account of the evolution of human cultural learning needs to show how that learning became critically important *prior* to the evolution of supporting adaptations for cultural learning, genetic or cultural. Once cultural learning reliably supports the transmission of skills critical for life success, there will be selection for genetic accommodation to make learning more reliable and/or less expensive. That sets up an enabling platform for positive feedback: more reliable social learning makes it possible for more information to flow through the social channel. In turn, if that information is important for a novice's life prospects, selection will favour genetic and cultural changes that make such learning more reliable or less effortful. That opens a possibility for further use of the social channel, and so on. Note though the "if" and "possibly". This is an engine that can stall. It depends on the importance of what is learned, the extent to which genetic adaptations improve learning efficiency, and the fitness rewards of increased efficiency. It might, for example, not impact fitness if a juvenile takes ten trials rather than twenty to learn how to turn embers into a functioning fire.

The establishment of extensive social learning without adaptations for social learning sounds like an impossible free lunch. But it is not. For one thing, adaptations for individual learning and for problem solving enhance social learning. Pliocene hominins were probably quite good at learning and problem solving. For learning is central to any lifeway that depends on both (i) flexibility: the exploitation of a wide-range of resources that varied over space and time; and (ii) high value, difficult to harvest resources. Harvest difficulty requires skill in locating, capturing and processing targets. Flexibility makes it impossible to pre-wire those skills. Furthermore, flexible foragers need a lot of information: they need to be competent over the full range of resources they exploit. Hominins evolved into highly flexible, high value, hard target foragers. Flexibility and a commitment to high value resources comes in degrees, and lifeways depending on these difficult resources evolved gradually in some hominin lineages in the Pliocene (Pickering and Dominguez-Rodrigo 2012). By the emergence of the habilines, around the Pliocene/Pleistocene boundary, the habilene lineage (at least) was morphologically committed to high value resources. Their lightly built teeth and jaws depended on access to such food (Wrangham 2009). We would expect those hominins to have competences that make them good learners, and many of those competences facilitate social as well as individual learning. That is true of executive control: the ability to retain focus, resist distraction. It is likewise true of the various forms of memory: working memory, semantic memory, episodic memory, muscle memory. Causal reasoning helps both individual and social learning: it helps the novice both anticipate and understand the results of another's action, when, say, he knaps a rock using a soft hammer. The same is true of a capacity to represent the environment using concepts defined by causal or functional similarities amongst the instances of that concept, rather than perceptual similarities. The concept of a hammer is such a concept: different hammers can look or feel quite different, and it's easier to learn about their importance if you can acquire such functionally-defined concepts. The bottom line is that we would expect transitional Pliocene-Pleistocene hominins, and early Pleistocene hominins, to be generally good at learning, compared to great ape baselines.

We have seen that those hominins had a lot to learn, as generalist flexible foragers targeting valuable but scattered elusive, cryptic or aggressive targets. Social input can reduce those burdens. (i) It can reduce the search space; if all you learn socially is the kind of rock to select for a tool, or where the right rock is to be found, you can focus your experimentation in the right place, or on the right stuff. (ii) Social input can substitute social signals of error—"Don't touch that"—for the world's signal of error. This does not always require explicit communication. For example, a juvenile might notice an adult's look of alarm at a novel sound. Informed adults often leak information, and alert juveniles can exploit that leakage. (iii) Social habits can make the arena of experimental learning safer. Frank Marlowe describes the Hadza practice of ensuring that a couple of adults stay at a band's overnight camp site (Marlowe 2010). This keeps predators away, making it safer for young children to explore in the local area. (iv) Attention to others' trials can distribute the costs of error over a group of peers, each learning from the others' mistakes (and successes) as well as their own. Even in cases where individual learning would be quite efficient, social learning is often faster or cheaper.

So the task is to explain how quite good general purpose learners became *committed* to social learning, and then became *adapted* for social learning. As we will see, as social learning became more efficient, it made material cooperation more profitable, and that reinforced selection for that efficient social learning. Three factors made the transition to commitment to social learning possible, prior to specific adaptations for cultural learning. First: as we have seen, good learners are decent at social learning. Second, social learning can be indirect. If offspring accompany their parents, their parents' choices of where to work and rest will structure the environment that their offspring explore through trial and error. Thus once making stone tools became a key component of habilene foraging, their accompanying children were exposed to the places in which raw material is to be found, and to that raw material. Third, just as a by-product of their economic activities, adults seed their offsprings' learning environments with informational resources. Much so-called social learning is actually hybrid learning: it is socially enhanced individual learning. Juvenile habilines will have the opportunity to play with failed and worn tools, with surplus tools (large numbers of flakes can be struck from a cobble), with tools not in use.

These factors build a platform for cultural learning, a platform that selects for cognitive and motivational factors more specific to cultural learning. Initially, these can be very simple. One is just tuning attention. Juveniles will learn more reliably if they find their parents' actions activities interesting, attending to them closely. Likewise, a small change in adult motivation—just greater tolerance of a close juvenile presence—would make them more effective information sources. These simple changes to motivation and attention make it possible for novices to exploit more of the information generated by adult actions. Second, the products of adult action are potential information resources: this is known as emulation learning. Third, and notoriously, so are the adults' actions themselves, even when they are just using their skills rather than demonstrating them. Chimps are not good at imitation learning—learning by attending to action sequences. But they can learn this way, and early hominins are unlikely to have been worse than chimps. Finally, adults can actively support learning, rather than merely tolerating juvenile presence. Peter Hiscock has suggested that active support probably has deep roots, for a competent guide sharply reduces the costs to a novice of learning to make stone tools, while imposing very modest costs on that guide (Hiscock 2014). This selects for the evolution of teaching. Moreover, to the extent that there are genetic adaptations driven by the importance of one specific skill (say: knapping), a platform is built for the social learning of other skills, not just the one whose importance drives the cognitive change. If juveniles are more attentive to adult behaviour, and watch their actions more closely, that improves their chances of learning anything those adults are capable of doing, not just their knapping. Likewise, if adults become more tolerant of inquisitive juveniles looking over their shoulder.

So the picture is one of the gradual, incremental growth of cultural learning, initially based on more general cognitive capacities; ultimately involving hominin minds tuned more specifically to cultural input. But the trajectory is driven initially by the indirect effects of adult lifeways structuring juvenile learning environments. These indirect effects are likely to aid the learning of any important, regularly repeated adult skill. If adults with juveniles regularly search out USOs these children will have many opportunities to watch their parents in action selecting likely plants, many opportunities to handle, smell and taste the above-ground stem and leaves, many opportunities to notice the places, and the kinds of places, where the plants are found. If the USOs need to be processed, once again there will be plenty of opportunities to notice (and to sample, if the adults are tolerant) the stages the USO goes through in its transition from plant to food. We know from ethnography that plant-based foraging, if it is to go beyond harvesting ripe fruit designed to be eaten, is informationally very demanding (Berlin 1992). Plant biodiversity is typically much more extensive than vertebrate diversity. Incautious experimentation can be very costly; and when resources are available to be harvested, the window of opportunity is often short (though that is less true with USOs, as not many other animals target them). In addition, ethnographically known forager range sizes are very much larger than those of great apes (see 3.2), and that was very probably true at least back to the erectines. Indeed, that is likely to be true of all the bipedal hominins, as the point of bipedality is efficient movement over space. This increases the botanical information foragers need, and the demands on spatial memory. Plant-based foragers need a good mental map of these large ranges, knowing where specific fruiting or seeding species are to be found, and when those foods are available. Juveniles very likely acquired this mental map, annotated with opportunities and risks, at least in part by regular movement through that territory guided by their parents, and perhaps with older and more experienced children. Foragers are not helicopter parents. Indeed, the ethnography of forager cultures suggests that forager children spend a lot of time in mixed age groups, exploring their environment with very little adult supervision (Lew-Levy, Reckin et al. 2017, Boyette and Hewlett 2018, Lew-Levy, Lavi et al. 2018, Lew-Levy, Kissler et al. 2020). Pleistocene adults, however, might have kept a closer eye on their children, given that they shared their world with an impressive array of predators.

The lesson we can draw from this is that even a very fortunate accidental innovation (as perhaps early stone tool-making was) can be stabilized, if that innovation is profitable enough to change adult behaviour enough to re-structure the juvenile learning environment. It is not difficult to imagine the kind of lucky accident that could alert a band to the value of USOs. A storm or a fallen tree could expose the storage organs at the soil surface. If that causes the band to subsequently systematically harvest them, they educate their young as a by-product of their own foraging. Innovations would still be fragile: their spread from their point of origin would depend on migrants shifting between groups being able to take the skill with them. Spread is far from automatic. In great ape societies, and so probably in early hominin societies as well, migration is outbreeding. In many cases, only adolescent females can move from their natal group. It is these young females who must take innovations with them. That is easier with fission-fusion organization, for then individuals or small groups forage independently through their range before coalescing at night camps. In such a social environment, a young female migrant can use her new foraging skills, because she can make decisions about where and how to forage, independently of the rest of the group. She can express her new skills. That is less likely, if the band as a whole moves and forages together. But even in fission-fusion regimes, until the innovation becomes part of routine regular activity, its transmission through social learning to the next generation will be chancy.

The upshot is that to the extent that social learning depends on indirect structuring of juvenile learning environments, established practices central to adult lifeways will probably be transmitted reliably to the next generation. But transmission will be coarse-grained: variations in adult skill levels, even if they make a real difference to task efficiency, are unlikely to be salient to the incoming generation. Moreover, innovations will rarely stabilize and spread. To stabilize at the point of origin the innovation has to re-organize adult lifeways enough to re-organize juvenile learning environments. To spread from the focal group of initial innovation, the innovating group must be connected to others. It follows that the number and the character of the connections between residential groups matters greatly to the spread of innovations. In contemporary forager societies, residential groups are open, with many adult-to-adult interactions across groups, making it possible for innovations to diffuse into a broader community. Great ape residential groups are more closed, primarily connected by sub-adult dispersal. That constrains diffusion. For an innovation to spread without adult to adult interaction, adolescents have to be competent and able to express their competence in their new social environment. As a consequence, innovations requiring cooperation (fishing or hunting with nets, for example) are particularly unlikely to spread by the diffusion of single sub-adults to neighbouring groups. Even when a migrant takes her new skill to a neighbouring group and expresses that skill, her practice must be regular and salient in that new environment to be a difference-maker for juvenile learning in the next generation.

The upshot is that in the earlier stages of hominin evolution, only innovations which females adopted and could use by themselves had much chance of spreading. That is true even if sub-adult males, not just sub-adult females, disperse from their natal group. As Ron Planer has pointed out to me, in fission-fusion environments, prior to the social recognition of paternity and the active involvement of fathers in their children, juveniles forage with their mother. Males do not have much effect on the rearing environment of their own children (and so if only sub-adult males disperse, the prospects of an innovation spreading are even poorer). Even if reproduction cooperation evolved with the emergence of the erectines (or earlier), the alternative carers of hominin infants were very likely mostly female: grandmothers, female relatives of the mother, perhaps adolescent females in the group learning the rudiments of infant care (Hrdy 2009). So female-linked innovations have a chance of spreading to neighbouring groups, though only if individuals determine their daily foraging routines. If bands travel and forage as a group, an adolescent immigrant would have little chance of influencing the band's habitual movement and activity patterns, and so it is unlikely that any novel skill could be expressed with the frequency and impact needed to change the learning experiences of juveniles in such a group. These considerations begin to explain the pattern noted in 1.2: the simultaneous dependence of hominins on a small set of socially learned, challenging skills and the very slow rate of innovation. For this pattern to break down, two quite different changes were needed. One was an increased efficiency of social learning within residential groups (perhaps with an increased innovation rate as well). That is the focus of the next section. The second is a change in interactions between residential groups: we turn to this in 3.1.

1.5 Cumulative Cultural Learning

Current and ethnographically known humans do not just learn culturally. As discussed briefly at the end of 1.1, our cultural learning is cumulative. We learn technologies and techniques we could never invent individually, capacities outside our ZLS. Moreover, some of those techniques and technologies are the result of multiple rounds of incremental improvement. As we saw in 1.1, Josep Call, Michael Tomasello and Claudio Tennie think that while great apes learn culturally, everything they learn is in their zone (Tennie, Call et al. 2009). That is not true of us. We learn culturally information and skills that as individuals we could not learn by our own unaided efforts. Sometimes our cultural learning takes us outside our ZLS, by giving us access to skills and technologies that are the result of repeated incremental improvements. Through the courtesy of Wulf Schiefenhövel, I recently had the chance to handle a recent stone axe from West Papua. It was a sophisticated tool. The cutting edge was made by controlled flaking and then grinding. The back of the head was shaped to fit the shaft, with the attachment secured by both bindings and adhesives. The haft itself was compound, with a shock absorber directly bound to the axe-head on one side (reducing the risk of fracture), and to the handle on the other. While we do not know the design history of this tool, very likely the ground edge, the reinforced bindings and the shock absorber are later additions to an initially simpler hafted axe. Many examples of pre-industrial, pre-metal technologies are almost certainly the result of multiple instances of progressive refinement. It is conceptually possible but vanishingly unlikely that the first stone tools made and used were Acheulian handaxes. Oldowan skills had to come first, and those skills were an essential foundation from which the Acheulian, and then later stone working techniques, developed. Similarly, it is almost certain that fire was domesticated in stages, with reliable ignition perhaps a million years later than the exploitation and partial control of naturally occurring fire (Gowlett 2016). Likewise, while I have no proof to offer, it is surely unlikely that an agent in need of an axe, but with no experience of axes, could invent from scratch an axe of the West Papuan design. The skill to make tools that are the result of incremental improvement are, almost always, outside our ZLS.[15]

Incrementally built capacities are a special case of escape from the human ZLS. But they are only a special case. To recycle my earlier example, foragers' natural history knowledge of their local patch is justly famous. These local data bases, often including the ability to recognize and characterize hundreds of species of plants and animals, are so extensive that it is vanishingly unlikely that any unaided individual could come to replicate this knowledge store. The challenge posed by the need to master local environmental information is its bandwidth: the sheer volume of information. While a novice could learn individually any single fact about the natural history of their local environment, they could not learn them all. Moreover, it is unlikely that a single generation could build this data base, especially in environments with a good deal of annual variation, where the patterns of animal and plant life are difficult to see. In cases like this, the crucial role of culture is to increase the efficiency of learning.

---

[15] The metaphor is vivid. But when applied to agents with the degree of cognitive plasticity of humans, it is somewhat misleading as well, as it can suggests that the ZLS is more or less the same for each agent, independently of their developmental environment.

This leads to a somewhat deflationary view of the cognitive capacities required for cumulative cultural learning. For there are many ways cultural inputs can increase the efficiency of individual learning, even without explicit instruction or demonstration. I think the same is true of the cultural transmission of the ability to make artefacts, like the Papua axe, that are the results of multiple cycles of improvement. The standard story is that incrementally improved technologies can be invented and passed on only by agents who learn by high fidelity imitation. The idea is that to exploit an incremental improvement, a novice needs to *notice* the difference between one person making the earlier version of a tool and another making the improved version. Having noticed that difference, they need to *adopt* the improved version.[16] It is true that cumulative cultural learning requires the reliable preservation and transmission of a group's informational resources from one generation to the next. But this does not require high fidelity imitation learning. Emulation is an alternative. Artefacts are templates. Novices can attend to the production sequence—to the expert's products rather than his/her actions; we will see this in Henrich's example of manioc processing, shortly. More generally, I think this line of thought understates the power of hybrid learning, socially supported exploration and error correction, to support the reliable transmission of skill and technology. No-one could invent a Papuan handaxe from scratch. But an agent who already has some skills in stone and wood working, allowed to handle an axe, and with time to experiment, might well manage. The difficulty of a specific learning task is relative to the repertoire of relevant skills already at the disposal of the novice, and some of these will be multi-purpose; acquired for one task, but useful for others.

---

[16] Alternatively, if the process of cumulative improvement does not depend on intelligent model choice by novices, but on the natural selection of variation existing in the population, children must attend so closely to the specific form of a skill expressed by a parent that they end up with that very form, and this too requires very high fidelity imitation learning.

So I agree that the difference between cultural learning and cumulative cultural learning is of great importance, and I likewise agree that our lineage has become uniquely dependent on cumulative cultural learning. Indeed, I shall shortly document that dependence. But I doubt that cumulative culture and the hominin escape from the ZLS depended on a specific upgrade in individual cultural learning capacity. It is noteworthy that the archaeological signature of cumulative culture appears gradually and unstably, and that is what we expect if cumulative culture at least initially depended on small improvements to a suite of existing capacities and on changes in the connectivity between residential groups.

Let's turn now though to a set of examples of cumulative culture. The aim is to illustrate both the fundamental importance of cumulative culture and the cognitive and social scaffolds of that culture. To continue with Tennie's metaphor, these are all examples of hominin forager capacities that are well outside their ZLS. I shall then discuss the cognitive and social supports of cumulative social learning, and how and when those supports were built. The examples include:

1. Those cases of trial and error learning that are very dangerous (or otherwise expensive); in the limit where errors are fatal. Learning about the edibility of mushrooms by trial and error requires great caution, to say the least. I remarked earlier that Peter Hiscock mounts a strong case that stone-working skills are remarkably dangerous to learn through individual experimentation, as misplaced strikes can cause razor-sharp shards to fly off at pace, in unpredictable directions (Hiscock 2014). Losing an eye is by no means impossible; deep and dangerous cuts are likely. He suggests that stone working skills were acquired not just by social learning but by active teaching. This was necessary, or close to necessary, to reduce those learning costs. Active teaching is cheap, with high benefits. The cost of experimentation, together with the difficulty of the target

skill, strongly suggests that Acheulian techniques were typically acquired with the active support of those who already had them.[17]

Another very clear ethnographic example, though much more recent, is oceanic navigation. Trial and error navigation between oceanic islands would be almost certainly suicidal, and some island cultures invest heavily in ensuring that these skills are passed on with due care and attention. One lovely example comes from the Marshall Islands, a scattered island archipelago in Oceania. The islands are almost all well and truly out of mutual sight; small islands, large ocean. Traditionally, navigation between them depended on both astronomical techniques and oceanic ones (there seems to be implicit directional information in the wave patterns). These skills were learned in part through guided experience as part of a crew, but also through elaborate and explicit teaching. This required purpose-built educational technology: stick and twine models of the wave patterns (Genz, Aucan et al. 2009). The challenges of oceanic navigation in the Pacific by traditional peoples without instruments are discussed more generally in (Lewis 1972).

2. Cases which are particularly error-intolerant: where there is only one way to solve a problem, and departures from that one right recipe are uninformative failures. Learning by experiment works best when an error suggests an appropriate correction, and the best solution can be found by successive approximation. A woman can use an inferior digging stick, though one with a sharper point, made from harder wood, with better weight, leverage and balance will be more

---

[17] Tennie and colleagues have recently suggested that early stone tool-making might be within the zone of latent hominin solutions. In response, the commentary on the paper points out that while they may be right about Oldowan technology, they much understate the profound differences between the Oldowan and the Acheulian skillset (Tennie, Premo et al. 2017).

efficient. She can learn with a rough prototype and gradually improve it, responding to specific inefficiencies in the next iteration. It is much more difficult to creep up on a good design for a composite tool like a bow in this way. Bindings can fail, the string can break, the wood can crack, the tip can detach, without these failures suggesting their remedy. Moreover, these failures will result in a bow that does not work at all, rather than an inferior but still useful one. Many forager technologies of the high northern latitudes are error-intolerant in multiple ways. Clothing has to fit; has to be weather-proof; has to be robust. The costs of failure are very high (Gilligan 2007b, Gilligan 2007a). Likewise, their vessels—kayaks and umiaks—are multi-component machines, and the components must be fitted together with precision, if the vessel is to be water-tight and balanced. Some of these cases are not just error-intolerant, the cost of error is high. A failure at sea is likely to be fatal, and the raw materials (hide, wood, bone) are all in limited supply. These are not factors that reward how-hard-can-it-be experimentation.

3. Joseph Henrich has pointed out that social learning is very important when the challenge is causally opaque. His most compelling example is manioc processing ((Henrich 2016) pp 58–59). Manioc (cassava) is both a good starch staple and one that can be grown well in marginal environments. But it needs to be detoxified, and making manioc safe is a protracted, laborious and deeply unintuitive process. It must be scraped, grated and washed to separate the fibre from the liquid. That liquid is then boiled, and the starch is left to rest for a few days. It can then be safely baked and eaten. At the beginning of this sequence, manioc is bitter and hence untempting, but the taste disappears before manioc is safe. (Again error costs are high too.) Starch sources are often chemically defended. Love describes the quite complex process of making pandanus kernels safe in his (Love 2009 (1936)). Likewise, cycad seeds are

large and prolific. These grow on my property and each seed cone can produce well over 10 kg of seed. But poison must be leached from the seeds (Beck 1992). This is a case where the causal recipe is passed on accurately, by emulation not imitation, but emulation in which the novice has access to each stage in the process, not just the finished product. The novice detoxifying manioc has to attend to the characteristics of manioc at each stage, but how the expert grates, pounds or soaks the pulp is irrelevant.

4. There are cases where bandwidth makes it virtually impossible for an individual to acquire a capacity by individual learning. This is the case I discussed earlier. Foragers know an enormous amount about their environment. Foragers can often identify hundreds of plant species. No individual can or could build such a local herbal unaided, just through acute observation and memory, given the other demands on time and energy. The cognitive capital of ethnographically known foragers is so great that no forager community could build it from scratch, even though each item is individually learnable. These resources are built by preservation from the previous generation and incremental additions. The same is probably true of much more ancient foragers. Rob Boyd and Pete Richerson rely on this class of examples to illustrate the fact that humans rely on cultural learning: they detail case after case of European explorers coming to miserable ends in places where the locals flourished with the aid of their accumulated informational capital.

5. Finally, and obviously, social learning is essential for learning the customs, norms, mores, rituals, language and material symbols of the community itself. That is particularly true as material symbols become more conventionalized and arbitrary, less iconic. With ethnographically known foragers, this cultural apparatus has high bandwidth and is causally opaque, so it is a special case, though an increasingly important one,

of Henrich's insight into the link between causal opacity and importance of social learning. Intuitive causal reasoning will rarely decipher the function of a ritual or the meaning of a particular pattern on a shield. One can guess and see what happens, but the costs of error will often be quite high, and the space of possible meanings is large. Indeed, Celia Heyes has argued that the main function of imitation learning is to learn the social signals of the community rather than its utilitarian skills (Heyes 2013).

From the Pliocene/Pleistocene boundary through to the very late Pleistocene, there was a transformation in the scope and fidelity of social learning and of the mechanisms that supported it. Perhaps with the exception of Oldowan technology, it is likely that Pliocene hominins learned socially, and hence more efficiently, information and skills that they could have learned individually. They probably relied largely on generalized learning capacities, on multi-functional cognitive mechanisms (like executive control), and on the indirect effects of adults on the learning environment of their children, perhaps supplemented by minor tweaks to juvenile attention and adult tolerance. Social learning depended on public information. By the emergence of *erectus*, a little after 2 mya, that was changing, but perhaps in relatively limited domains. Acheulian technology is some evidence of that, as perhaps is evidence of the first steps in the control of fire. So too is evidence of ambush hunting at about 1.8 mya. That implies an archaeologically invisible technology of wooden spears (and probably other soft materials technology). But more importantly, it implies that erectines understood the natural history and likely responses of their target animals. Hunting larger animals with short range weapons depends on an intimate understanding of game and habitat (Binford 2007). Moreover, ambush hunting implies some ability to communicate to coordinate. Hunting largish animals with short range weapons relies on coordination as well as expertise. Bandwidth is going up, and if erectines coordinated using a simple protolanguage, the cultural learning of arbitrary social codes had gained a foothold. Later in the Pleistocene, human lifeways depended on a river of information flowing between the generations, and adult competence depended on capacities that could only be acquired socially.

1.6 Adapted Minds and Environments

So over perhaps 3–4 million years, cultural learning has gone from being a useful adjunct to individual learning to a dominating feature of human development. What features made this transformation possible, and when did they emerge? I doubt that cumulative social learning depended on a single key innovation. For there is no threshold-like change in the record. Rather, this dominating role of cultural learning depended on the slow construction of cognitive, social, developmental and material supports. The ingredients that supported this much expanded version of cultural learning include:

Encephalization and Its Consequences. I assume one factor was the general expansion of neural resources as hominins became increasingly encephalized through the erectus-Heidelbergensis-late Pleistocene grades. These extra resources enhanced general purpose and multi-functional capacities already available, in much more attenuated versions, to Pliocene hominins. These probably included memory, causal reasoning, executive control, theory of mind and the like. That said, it is rather striking that there is no clean correlation between the extent of encephalization and archaeological signals of technical, ecological or social complexity.

Life History. Arguably, hominin life history changed in two relevant ways. One was a trend to increased adult lifespan, and the linked extension of time as a juvenile. *Erectus* shows some sign of this trend. The Nakatasome Boy was just about sexually mature at a little over 12, but that was probably a slower life history than that of *habilus* or the australopithecines, and there is some signal of the characteristic AMH pattern of the childhood slowdown in body growth while brain development continues ((Maslin 2017) pp 32–34). The longer the period of juvenile support and protection, the more resources that juvenile has for learning. Michael Gurven, Hillard Kaplan and their colleagues argue that (at least for AMHs) the leisurely stroll to adulthood is an adaptation to the demanding bandwidth of social learning, and is made possible by positive feedback between adult foraging efficiency and extensive social learning (Gurven, Kaplan et al. 2006, Kaplan, Gangestad et al. 2007, Kaplan, Hooper et al. 2009); for a recent review, see (Koster, McElreath et al. 2020). Adult efficiency makes long dependence affordable, and the extensive education flowing from long dependence makes foragers efficient. Ethnographic evidence suggests that this economic support allows forager children to be free range and self-directed, learning a lot from one another (the contrast with the children of subsistence farmers is very marked). But the same evidence shows that this organisation of childhood is a remarkably reliable and low-cost pathway to adult competence (Lew-Levy, Reckin et al. 2017, Boyette and Hewlett 2018).[18]

In addition to the longer juvenile span, in somewhat different ways Sarah Hrdy, Carel van Schaik and Kristin Hawkes (and their various colleagues) have suggested that hominins were cooperative breeders. Hawkes identified grandmothers as the crucial source of support. Hrdy thinks that allomothering was variably distributed over relatives, social allies, and adolescents in need of experience, and perhaps even fathers. On either view, reproductive cooperation

---

[18] The view that slow life history is an adaptation making possible a long education is controversial and is (inevitably) based on a small sample of cases. The alternative is that the long period as a juvenile is a side effect of selection for large body size: bigger bodies take longer to grow. Even if that is right, long dependence affords the opportunity of very extensive learning.

enhances social learning, both by providing young children with access to more models, and by selecting more generally for adult tolerance of infants, and infant responsiveness to adults. Again, it is probable that this evolutionary shift began or accelerated with erectus (Opie and Power 2008), beginning the trend towards large-headed babies, challenging at birth and utterly dependent thereafter (Hawkes and Bird 2002, Hawkes 2003, Hrdy 2009, Hawkes and O'Connell 2010).

New Cognitive Architecture. One possibility is that the Pleistocene saw the evolution of novel (or massively transformed) cognitive capacities, either specialized for social learning or powerfully enhancing social learning. Language and theory of mind are obviously pivotal in many social contexts. Equally obviously, they enhance social learning. Language is a medium of unparalleled power in conveying information about the elsewhere, for passing on the lore of accumulated experience, and for making salient subtle differences between kinds by naming them differently. Likewise, theory of mind is relevant. The expert-novice transaction is more efficient if the novice understands what the expert is trying to do, and the expert understands what the novice does and does not know. To demonstrate a skill, as distinct from displaying it, to guide practice or correct errors, an expert has to represent her own skill to herself, and that is a metarepresentational task. Imitation learning and Gergely and Csibra's "natural pedagogy hypothesis" are candidate cognitive mechanisms supposedly specialized for social learning (Csibra and Gergely 2009, Csibra and Gergely 2011). Almost everyone agrees that human cognitive architecture has been shaped by adaptations for social learning. The problem is to locate the origin and expansion of these capacities in the historical record. In particular, if the Pleistocene expansion of social learning depended predominantly on cognitive adaptations for social learning, we would expect to see, as these capacities evolved incrementally, a smooth and incremental upward trend in the results of social learning. But we do not: we see lots of apparent stasis and reversals, as capacities appear and disappear from the record. The record of fire is an instance of this pattern.[19]

Celia Heyes' scepticism might be instructive here. She does not doubt the current importance of language, imitation, theory of mind and the like for social learning. But she thinks these cognitive gadgets are themselves the product of social learning; of cultural rather than genetic evolution. Heyes' picture would lead us to expect a long lag time before social learning takes-off. For on Heyes' picture, the tools which power take-off had to be built, presumably slowly and inefficiently, with cognitive and learning capacities not yet specialized for high bandwidth, high fidelity social learning. We have to learn socially how to learn socially, and to do so without tools specifically adapted for that task (Heyes 2012, Heyes 2018). On this picture, we might expect the explosion of social learning to have a very long fuse, as the cognitive gadgets which make us efficient social learners had to be built by cultural evolution, without cognitive capacities specialized for that task. But once the platform had been built, take-off would be rapid.

Cognitive Scaffolds. Even if Heyes' scepticism about the existence of genetically based cognitive adaptations for cultural learning is extreme, much contemporary social learning undeniably depends on culturally constructed devices. These include libraries and other external stores of information; depictions in two or three dimensions: diagrams, maps and models; notation systems; specialized technical vocabularies. Moreover, we have got better at using scaffolds like these, through culturally evolved lore on how to use these tools as we acquire critical information and skills. Is this a feature only of contemporary life, or might social learning in the Pleistocene been scaffolded by artefacts? I think scaffolds (both physical devices and social practices) that enhance learning have a Pleistocene history. It is certainly true that artefact-scaffolded

---

[19] Of course, it could still be true that specialist capacities are important but not sufficient.

learning is found in small scale societies. We have already seen that Marshall Islanders teach navigation with the aid of models of sea flow, and this is not an isolated example, for foragers quite often provide their children with miniaturised tools (Lew-Levy, Reckin et al. 2017). Lynne Kelly details the extensive use of physical scaffolds (masks and much else) in teaching ritual knowledge in Aboriginal Australia. Importantly, Kelly argues that crucial ecological information is carried in these ritual narratives, built into easy to learn, easy to remember stories (Kelly 2015).[20] Moreover, as Dan Dennett pointed out long ago, an artefact does not have to be purpose-built for learning in order to aid learning. A spear can serve as a template for making another spear. Finally, while we have no firm dates for the evolution of language, surely it is not *very recent*, as it is common to our whole species. Language powers social learning. Amongst much else, a lexicon is a teaching tool (Dennett 1993). Labels make subtle differences and unobvious similarities more salient. On my bush property, there are three species of thornbill, distinguished by very subtle differences in plumage, voice and behaviour. It would be very difficult to notice that there were in fact three species of these unobtrusive, small brown birds without the different species labels to clue you in to the fact that there were stable differences to notice. Their natural environment matters to foragers, and so the languages of small scale societies have technical vocabularies congruent with their technologies and ecological resources (for an account of the coevolution of language with other features of hominin life, see Planer and Sterelny forthcoming).

Adapted Learning Environments. While there is a noisy and fractious consensus on the fact that hominin minds are adapted for cultural learning, there is less attention to the equally important fact that hominin developmental environments are adaptive for cultural learning. Some of those adaptive effects are side-effects. As we have seen, adults structure the environments that their children

---

[20] Though see (Hiscock 2020) for a sceptical response.

explore in ways that promote the acquisition of important skills. To those who look and notice, adult actions are rich in useful information: catching and collecting; making and preparing. And in forager life, a lot of adult actions are in public. There is not a lot of private space in forager camps (Hewlett, Hudson et al. 2019) (though in some forager societies there is some sex segregation). Information also leaks from adult conversations. One example is forager camp fire conversations about the day's hunting; this is a very pervasive feature of forager life, and foragers are very tolerant of children's presence at adult activities. Less obviously, forager economic interests adaptively structure juvenile learning, not just through exposure but because forager children are encouraged to contribute to their own upkeep, as soon as it is moderately safe for them to do so (for a case study, see (Bock 2005); for a general review, see (Lew-Levy, Reckin et al. 2017)). In encouraging them to begin providing for themselves, it is optimal both for adult economic interests and the juvenile's developmental trajectory for the adult to encourage activities at the edge of their children's current competence. If they attempt tasks well beyond their reach, that will be futile or dangerous. But stretching them near their limits gets the most from their foraging, reducing the burden on adult provisioning, while adaptively structuring their practice in the acquisition of adult skills. But while some of the adaptive structure is a side-effect, a good deal is teaching, broadly construed. Forager toys are often weapons in miniature (for a selection of Australian examples, see (Haagen 1994)). Games rehearse and prepare for adult skills. It is common for boys to accompany their father on hunts as soon as they can walk far enough (usually at about 12), even though they will not be much use on the hunt. There is also a good deal of explicit teaching, especially of ritual knowledge (Meggitt 1962).

Importantly, some small scale societies have apprentice traditions, closely analogous to the craft guilds of Medieval and Early Modern Europe, where skill is transmitted from expert to novice by structuring the learning environment, by scaffolding learning by giving the novice an appropriate sequence of tasks, so one episode of learning builds on the last, by seeding the learning environment with informative material resources, and with support from peers. Mostly these pedagogical arrangements are very informal, with relatively little explicit teaching (except of ritual). But not always. Two examples are stone adze making in New Guinea (Stout 2002) and navigation in the Marshalls. Joseph Henrich and Francisco Gil-White suggest that a distinctive form of human status difference has evolved as a result of these apprentice-like interactions: a hierarchy of prestige. Novices show deference and grant status in return for advice and guidance (Henrich and Gil-White 2001). In sum, then, forager lifeways support forager children's education in many mutually supporting ways.

Social Environment. The discussion of apprentice-structured learning environments and of the role of reproductive cooperation focuses on the immediate social environment of the novice. The more global environment is also relevant to the reliability and power of social learning. In particular, social scale matters: both the size of the residential group itself, and its connections to other groups; connections that allow them to pool information. Adam Powell and colleagues have stressed the importance of size. Bigger is better, because novices have access to more models, probably including more expert models, just through natural variation. Size offers redundancy, buffering the community against the risk of loss of information through unfortunate accidents to its experts (Powell, Shennan et al. 2009). This risk is not trivial. Connection buffers this risk in similar ways. If adults, not just juveniles, can move fairly freely between residential groups, the total informational resources of the community are buffered. Likewise, the prospects of an innovation spreading and establishing are improved. For any innovation that is confined to a single band is very vulnerable to demographic accident. Thus the emergence of recognized and stabilized kinship networks and social alliances across distinct residential groups, and the practice of overnight camps assembling into larger communities at times of seasonal plenty, were both important to the take-off of cumulative culture. Indeed as noted at the end of 1.4, until networks of interconnected bands emerge, with fairly free movement between them, innovations, which are the fuel of accumulation, are unlikely to stabilize.

Size also makes specialization possible (Ofek 2001). A band of 15 is unlikely to be able to support, say, a specialist bowyer. A community of 150 (or a well-networked cluster of smaller bands) might. Specialization improves skill level, and perhaps also the rate of innovation. Not only are specialists more skilled; it is worth their while to invest in and improve specialist equipment. A forager who fishes once a year would be unwise to pay the costs of making a fishing net. A forager who regularly fishes might well find that profitable. Rather more controversially, it has been argued that cultural learning is more efficient in larger communities. Here is the idea. In any form of knowledge transfer, there is a risk of error creeping in. The more difficult a skill is to learn, the greater the risk. Size (the argument goes) mitigates this risk, for there is more natural variation of talent in larger groups. With more expert models, and more talented novices, there is a better chance that information loss can be prevented or corrected. Joseph Henrich, Adam Powell and their colleagues have developed this line of thought with the aid of formal models, and applied those models to the archaeological record, putting formal detail on the basic idea that bigger is better, because more talented novices have access to more models, including more expert models (the idea is controversial, see (Sterelny 2020-a) for discussion and review).

Cumulatively, these considerations from redundancy, specialization and cultural learning efficiency predict that increases in size or connection should covary with the more reliable retention and improvement of informational capital.

1.7 Overview

The archaeological record suggests the following picture. There was a very long period, perhaps even dating from the habilines, but certainly from the erectines, in which social learning was essential to the cooperative foraging of high value targets, foraging on which Pleistocene hominins depended. This supported the acquisition of skill and information that was not within the hominin ZLS. Essential skills had to be acquired socially: these hominins stood on the shoulders of their predecessors. But bandwidth was narrow. Though cultural learning was cumulative, it was so in a rather minimal way. Even so, it was important, for it contributed essential skills that made collective action profitable. However, the scope of social learning was not increasing, nor were traditions within its scope fine-tuned and upgraded. If we date this limited version of cumulative culture only from the origins of the Acheulian, this period lasted about 1.5 million years, though with increasing signs of change from about 800 kya. Moreover, the technological stasis of the Acheulian should not be overstated. For one thing, we do not know the developments in soft material technology. For another, fire was added to material culture. Third, the shift into more temperate areas suggests that technique and environmental understanding was improving, perhaps in conjunction with increased encephalization through this period. Furthermore there is some suggestion that technique in the late Acheulian was more refined (see 1.3). Even so, it seems that innovations rarely spread beyond the social circle of origin, and hence that accumulation was sharply constrained, though perhaps 1 million years is a safer estimate of this period of sharp constraint.

The MSA (roughly 300 kya–100 kya) seems to have been unstable in this respect. We do see striking innovations in the archaeological record: new materials; new methods of stone working; new kinds of tools; early evidence of material symbols; grindstones and other evidence of an expanding resource base. Indeed, there are hints of some of these techniques even earlier, at about 500 kya (Wilkins and Chazan 2012, Wilkins, Schoville et al. 2012). But often these innovations are not continuous in time and space; microliths appear in one place, disappear and re-appear somewhere else, tens of thousands of years later. Even fire has a record like this between 800 and 200 kya. We should not over-interpret this record. These gaps may show an innovation establishing locally, but then lost because social transmission is not yet fully reliable. But apparent gaps may just be failures of preservation. Even if real, they can reflect economic changes rather than losses of capacity. For example, Peter Hiscock (writing of a much later time) argues that Tasmanian Aboriginals abandoned fishing as wallaby hunting became more profitable, not because they forgot how to fish (Hiscock 2008). Nonetheless, the overall impression is that these more recent MSA hominins were still at risk of serious losses of their informational capital.

From about 100 kya, while there are still innovations followed by temporary disappearances, the rate of change and diversification picks up as the Pleistocene draws to a close. These very late Pleistocene foragers seem to have the same capacities for cumulative social learning as ethnographically known forager populations. The natural thought is that gene-culture coevolution over the Acheulian and into the MSA had built very large-brained humans (AMHs, Neanderthals, Denisovans) that had some genetically based cognitive adaptations for social learning. Over the last 300 k years, and in an increasing trend, the power of those adaptations was much enhanced by a combination of culturally learned cognitive skills for cultural learning, cultural and physical scaffolds which support cultural learning, developmental environments which supported, encouraged and rewarded social learning, and changes in social network structure. And, of course, possibly further refinements of genetic adaptations for cultural learning. These all made it easier for a local group to retain and improve its informational resources, and made it more likely for an innovation to spread from its local group to establish regionally.

Hominin social learning originally depended on the exploitation of public information.[21] As hominins, perhaps around the Pliocene/Pleistocene boundary began to exploit richer resources using more demanding technology, adult foraging generated more public information. But selection also began to favour a more active role by adults, and a more focussed response from novices. Both Acheulian technology and large game hunting depended on a lot of learning, and it would be difficult (perhaps impossible) for agents to acquire the skills and information they needed by unguided experimentation. That is especially true if Hiscock is right about the high error costs in learning to make stone tools without guidance. The same is probably true of much gathering, which depends on a rich ethnobotany. Moreover, these learned capacities were indispensable. Through much of the Pleistocene, forager lifeways depended on ecological cooperation where success depended on cross-generational information sharing (no doubt with some within-generation sharing too). The more foragers learned about their local habitat, the more they could profit from it, often acting in concert. The profits from successfully harvesting local resources supported the demographic and life history factors that made intergenerational information flow reliable. That flow, and the profits it made possible, began to increase in the late Pleistocene as the demographic environment, the learning niche of young Pleistocene hominins, and the onboard cognitive resources of those young hominins jointly boosted the chances of a local community preserving and increasing their informational resources.

This chapter has focussed on the role of culture in providing the tools that make cooperation profitable, and on some of the constraints on intergenerational cultural flow that limited the expansion of that repertoire for most of hominin history. The role of

---

[21] I have in mind information with a long shelf life. Chimps produce alert and warning vocalizations about important but transient phenomena, and almost certainly so did Pliocene hominins.

culture in powering the generation of benefit does not disappear in the next two chapters: the advantages of specialization and the division of labour enter in the next chapter, and the possibilities opened up by larger scale collective action are an important theme of chapter 3. These too require skills (like a richer language) and institutions (like kinship systems) that are built by cumulative cultural evolution. But the stability of cooperation, and the ways stability is threatened by greater social complexity become important in the next chapters. These complexities include greater differentiation within bands and communities, increases in social scale, and increases in agents' investments in the future, as their planning horizons expanded from hours and days to weeks, months, years.

2
The Pleistocene Social Contract

2.1 Free-Riders and Bullies

Chapter 1 was about the role of culture, and especially cultural learning, in supercharging the profits of cooperation. Those profits were amplified by the use of physical tools, and of expertise, both increasingly dependent on cultural learning. In addition, they were amplified by the invention and social transmission of cultural tools for communication (most obviously language and its ancestors). Communication makes coordination possible, especially coordination across time and space, between agents out of eyeshot and earshot, as ambush hunting might require. Moreover, these tools of communication made it possible for social worlds to emerge that were both large enough and yet connected enough for cooperative risk management, to buffer and protect cognitive capital, and for agents to enjoy the first benefits of specialization and the division of labour. Foragers developed networks of connection that enable them to respond when local conditions became difficult by moving to where they had friends and allies, and these reciprocation networks depend on mutual recognition of rights and responsibilities. The Hxaro gift exchange system of !Kung bushmen[1] is a classic example of such a system of reciprocal insurance (Wiessner 2002a). But similar systems are widespread amongst mobile forager

---

[1] These bushmen have customs through which an individual in one band will have a range of personal, individual connections to other bands; ties maintained by regular, mutual gifts and visits, and these in turn guarantee a hospitable reception if strife and trouble require an agent to move from his usual band and patch. These networks can be quite extensive, connecting an individual to several other bands (Wiessner 2014).

cultures. Keen's survey of Australian indigenous cultures at contact shows that individuals in one community typically had kin or ritual connection to other communities, giving them some access rights (Keen 2004).

However, as noted in 1.1, it is not enough for cooperation to be profitable. The distribution of its profits must encourage further cooperation. If cooperative acts have costs, as they often do, there must be mechanisms that make it likely that all who profit pay approximately their share of those costs. There are two forms of cheating in a cooperative world: not paying your fair share of the costs of a cooperative enterprise (free-riding) and hijacking more than your share of the profits (bullying and greed). Of course it is possible to be both a free-rider and a bully: lions sometimes seem to do both, leaving the actual hunting to the lionesses, and then taking a larger share of the kill (Scheel and Packer 1991). Unchecked, both have the potential to cause cooperative arrangements to collapse, as free-riding increases the costs of cooperating to the co-operators, and bullying reduces its profits, so there comes a tipping point where co-operators do best to cease cooperating and go it alone. Of the two forms of cheating, bullying is potentially the most destabilizing: a bully can monopolize the whole profit of an enterprise, while free-riding can only increase the costs of cooperating, proportionate to the number of co-operators. So, for example, in a group of five an agent who fully free-rides inflates each co-operator's costs from 20% to 25% of the total effort.[2] I will use "cheating" or "defecting" as general terms to cover free-riding, bullying and various hybrids of the two.

These barriers to stable cooperation are important: they help explain why cooperation is so limited, especially between agents who are not closely related. Chimpanzees cooperate, but in very limited

---

[2] Much of the modelling work on the evolution of cooperation does not distinguish between these threats to cooperation, and nearly all of the experimental work in behavioural economics is focused on free-riding. So there is something of a gap in theory here.

ways. Male chimps cooperate in patrolling the boundaries of their territory, and, when they can, opportunistically killing vulnerable males of adjoining groups. In this form of cooperation, there is not much temptation to cheat. They do not attack unless the odds are so favourable (4:1) that the attackers risk little (Wrangham 1999). The benefits—weakening the perennially hostile adjoining group—are distributed automatically. Chimps also collectively hunt colobus monkeys. There is some doubt as to whether this is genuinely cooperative, or whether the chimps form a mob in which each chimp aims to maximize his chances of making the kill. Certainly, the chimp that does make the kill gets more of the meat than any other, but begging and harassment by the others result in some sharing out. To the extent that this is cooperative, it does not generate much temptation to cheat. Hunts are not planned; they are the result of accidental encounters that catch monkeys in a situation of risk. There is no real risk in taking part, nor much opportunity cost. Moreover, there is always a chance of being lucky, making the kill. So amongst chimps, most cooperation is low-risk. An exception might be joining a coalition aiming to depose the current alpha; that may involve genuine risk. But power coalitions amongst chimps are small, and quite often link brothers, and these are both factors that help stabilize cooperation.

The social world of the chimps is inconsistent with most of the profitable forms of cooperation that characterized the lives of the erectines and more recent hominins (and perhaps of more ancient ones). Chimps live in a social world of bullying: they live in social worlds with a quite marked dominance hierarchy. At its peak is an alpha male, often relying on support from another powerful male (support which is paid for by direct reciprocation, and tolerance of the key ally's mating advances). Aggression flows down the hierarchy; submission and fear flow up. Hence chimps, like all great apes, are feed-as-you-go foragers. Central place foraging would not be stable in a chimp-like social world. Harvesting food at one place and taking it to a safer, collective campsite for processing and consumption is not a stable strategy if those that return with food risk being dispossessed. One might need to take, say, honey away from a hive to eat it in safety, but it would be unwise for a subordinate to return with honey to a joint camp. In a bully-dominated social world, the richer the food being bought to camp, the greater the risk those higher in rank will just take it.[3] Hawkes' helpful grandmother could not count on being able to provision her daughter's weanlings. For she would be at risk of dispossession from any adult or near-adult male (Hawkes, O'Connell et al. 1998, O'Connell, Hawkes et al. 1999). The more successful her foraging, the greater her risk. The same is true of investment in artefacts. There is no profit in spending time and energy making a well-made tool if it is likely to be pirated by a more dominant individual. The better the tool, the greater the risk of its being taken. All the great apes live in dominance-structured social worlds (though perhaps the bonobos, less so). So it is very likely that the Last Common Ancestor of the *pan* and *hominin* lineages did too. Sometime in the Pliocene or early Pleistocene, there was a first critical transformation in hominin cooperation. The great ape pattern was broken; the dominance hierarchy was suppressed, no doubt at first unstably and partially. But that suppression opened the door to forms of cooperation that are profitable, but which would be unstable in an environment where bullying expropriation was a serious and persistent threat.

Picking up from the discussion at the end of 1.1, I shall suggest that the establishment of a social order of relatively egalitarian, mutualist social bands was the first of four transitions in the character of hominin cooperation. A second, in the late Pleistocene, was a change in the economic basis of cooperation from immediate return mutualism to one in which direct and indirect reciprocation played an important role. This was perhaps between 120 kya and 50 kya, at different times in different places. The third and fourth concern changes in the complexity and scale of human social life.

---

[3] That may be why female chimps do not normally join monkey hunts: they would be too likely to have their catch pirated, were they to make the kill.

In 1.6, I discussed the importance of social scale, and the transition from life in the relatively closed social world of a great ape residential group to the richly connected forager bands of ethnography. There is reason to suspect that this transition was very gradual. Its initial roots may date back to the Heidelbergensians, at about 800 kya. But it was not complete until the very late Pleistocene (perhaps even later). For it is only then that we find evidence of active cooperation across residential groups, and perhaps of clan structures that transcend an individual forager band. The final transition began in the terminal Pleistocene (about 25 kya–12 kya) and in the early Holocene, with the origins of sedentary society. This led to an increase in social scale and social inequality. In trying to understand why cooperation is stable, scale, complexity and inequality all matter. For mechanisms that suffice to stabilize cooperation in small politically unstructured and relatively homogenous social environments breakdown in larger and more structured ones. Personal knowledge and trust can stabilize cooperation in small, intimate social environments but not larger and more differentiated ones. Continued cooperation is especially puzzling in social worlds that are not just larger but also hierarchically structured. For these seem to be cases where the profits of cooperation are largely hijacked by elites. In such cases, theory predicts the collapse of cooperation. The take-home message of this chapter is that culturally evolved tools—language, myth, ritual, explicit norms[4]—play a central role in the stability of cooperation in the late Pleistocene shift in the economic foundations of cooperation, and an equally central role in the survival of the social contract through the final Pleistocene and early Holocene social revolutions. The four-stage picture is summarised in Table 2.1. This chapter focusses on the first two of these transitions; the others are reserved for later chapters.

---

[4] Gene-culture coevolution probably played a central role in our capacity to respond to myth and ritual, to use language, to understand and respond to norms. But the versions of language, myth, ritual and norm that characterize particular communities are preserved, modified and transmitted by cultural learning.

Table 2.1 Transitions in Hominin Cooperation

Transition	Key Feature of Social Organization	Cultural Innovations That Supported the Transition	Very Approximate Dates	Form of Cooperation
From largely independent foraging to immediate return mutualism.	Suppression of male dominance hierarchy.	Weapons. Perhaps improved communication & coordination. Coalitions; later, sustained coalitions.	1.8 mya–800 kya (from early erectus to the evolution of Heidelbergensis)	Collective scavenging + hunting. Home base foraging (hence greater role for female reproductive cooperation). Investment in tools rational.
Indirect reciprocation becomes important	Good reputation essential to life prospects	Gossip: language advanced enough to make reputation reliable. Explicit norms. Expanded role for ritual in strengthening social bonds/ easing social tensions.	120 kya–50 kya	Exploitation of a much broader resource portfolio. More efficient use of territory. Risk management through reciprocation. First potentials for specialization, and division of labour.

(*continued*)

Table 2.1 Continued

Transition	Key Feature of Social Organization	Cultural Innovations That Supported the Transition	Very Approximate Dates	Form of Cooperation
Cooperation across bands. Collective action and cooperation at community level.	Bands nested within a larger group, ultimately the formation of clan-like organizations transcending individual bands.	Elaborated kinship systems (sometimes with clan-like organization). Formalized reciprocation relations between individuals in distinct bands. Ritual life asserts collective identity in response to others: signalling outward, not just to one another.	Probably beginning with Heidelbergensians. But not complete until very late Pleistocene. Even then not universal in forager cultures.	Information flow across bands. Demographic buffering. Risk management across bands. Large scale collective action. Collective action with high costs, perhaps including war.
Cooperation in sedentary, complex, and hierarchical societies.	Formal and informal leadership positions. Significant and enduring differences in material wealth. Interactions often mediated by social role rather than direct mutual knowledge.	Property rights. Quasi-legal institutions; i.e., norms of action linked to norms of enforcement. Forager norms of sharing transformed into norms of entitlement & status.	Beginning at the very end of the Pleistocene/early Holocene	Great expansion of specialization and exchange. Great expansion of the scale of collective action. Shift towards the "cooperation with strangers" of mass society.

2.2 Curbing Dominance Hierarchies

One of the robust findings in both the theoretical and experimental work on cooperation is that it erodes rapidly in the face of unchecked cheating (Fehr and Gachter 2002, Fehr and Fischbacher 2003, Gintis, Henrich et al. 2008). This work has a presupposition that will be important in chapter 4: those currently cooperating have some non-cooperative, go-it-alone alternative. That might not be true: the lone wolf option might be excluded by overwhelming coercive power; by hostile neighbours or by peculiarities of the local ecology. It is one thing to be a lone wolf; another, to be a lone sheep. Even so, evidence large game hunting, and hence of a well-established cooperative life at or before the migration of the erectines through much of the old world is a reliable signal that cheating was under control. As noted in 2.1, in turn that implies that dominance did not determine the flow of resources in Pleistocene bands.

We do not know how or when bullies were stripped of their coercive power in the hominin lineage, though as noted earlier, this was at least in progress in the early Pleistocene. There is some evidence that male/male competition was becoming less important in the Pliocene (and evidence of intense male-male competition is a signature of dominance-structured societies). Sexual dimorphism of body size became less marked, and male and female dentition became more similar (male chimps have more pronounced canines than females, and so perhaps did early australopithecines (Manthi, Plavcan et al. 2012)).

There is, however, a plausible model of this transition, one which has the potential to explain why late Pliocene or Pleistocene hominins could suppress expropriation of cooperation's profits by bullies, whereas chimps could not (and hence have few or no cooperation profits to distribute). The model consists of three elements:

1. An initial specialization in a form of cooperation which was profitable and where the problem of detecting and policing cheating was relatively tractable.
2. The evolution of the use of weapons. Paul Bingham has argued that the evolution of weaponized violence was sufficient to explain the establishment of egalitarian forager life (Bingham 1999, Bingham 2000). His picture is too simple, but he has an important insight: weapons make a coalition of the weaker against the strongest potentially deadly for the alpha.
3. The evolution of both greater social intelligence and greater impulse control, in hominins as compared to great apes.

Let's begin with the form of cooperation that was less vulnerable to cheating. In 1.3, I noted that there is persuasive evidence of erectine large- and medium-game hunting from about 1.8 mya. In itself, this is a signature of cooperation, since the prospects of a single individual killing an ungulate with a thrown wooden spear (or stabbing spear) are remote. Henry Bunn and Travis Pickering argue (I think persuasively) that erectines probably hunted from ambush (Pickering 2013). That requires spears; excellent natural history knowledge, to site the ambush point properly, and impulse control of high order, since the hunters must wait in cover, quietly, and often for hours. They cannot afford to alarm birds and other animals, for if alarmed, their calls can alert their target. If others in the band are required to drive the targets past the ambush point, planning and coordination are needed as well. All this implies a considerable evolutionary prequel of small game hunting and (very likely) power scavenging, building the weapons skills,[5] expertise and impulse control needed for ambush hunting.

[5] Pickering points out that one chimp group uses very simple spears to hunt bushbabies, and that there is a very smooth incremental pathway from these simple stick spears through to multi-component, woomera-launched javelins (Pickering and Bunn 2012). There is some debate about the relative importance of small-game hunting versus scavenging in the evolutionary prequel to ambush hunting (see (Thompson, Carvalho et al. 2019)). The analysis offered here is neutral on this issue.

This form of cooperation is profitable, and yet poses less severe problems in detecting and deterring cheats. Michael Tomasello has pointed out that power scavenging (that is, driving predator from its kill rather than just inheriting its leavings) and ambush hunting are immediate return mutualisms (Tomasello, Melis et al. 2012, Tomasello 2016). The profits of cooperation are generated immediately (the kill is seized; the ambush is successfully sprung), and they are (or can be) divided on the spot. This contrasts with a form of cooperation which has often been the focus of evolutionary theory, reciprocation, in which one agent makes some contribution to others' welfare in the expectation that this contribution will be returned with profit in the future, either by those directly helped (direct reciprocation) or others (indirect reciprocation). The first mover in a reciprocation game is clearly vulnerable to cheating. For reasons that I explore in the next section, in economies of reciprocation, detecting and policing cheating are motivationally and cognitively challenging. Immediate return mutualism of the kind exemplified by (say) power scavenging is not immune to the danger of cheating. But cheating that *seriously* impacts on the costs or returns of others will be obvious, especially any attempt to expropriate a destabilizingly disproportionate share of the kill. All of those that drove (say) the leopard from the kill are there. What each tries to take will be obvious to all. No doubt, and especially in the early stages of this trajectory, the division will be a scrambling squabble, with much hacking and tearing off of chunks. Even so, any attempt to claim a near-monopoly, would be (i) obvious to all the others; (ii) a threat, equally, to the interests of all the others; (iii) a stimulus to resentment and anger. And while after a successful hunt, there is probably not much temptation to monopolize a kill, that may not be true of a kill pirated from other predators, for that would depend on how much of the kill was left.

In a resentful and volatile group, there is every prospect of anger spreading by emotional contagion and erupting as collective violence. Frans de Waal's ethnographic descriptions of chimp society include accounts of spontaneous, infectious outbursts of anger at dominance; an angry mob temporarily suspending the established order of power, as an alpha is put to flight. Contagious anger is dangerous to its target. In chimp society these occasional storms blow over without making any significant difference to the distribution of resources (material, sexual, political) in chimp life. Moreover, chimps lack both the incentive and the cognitive, emotional and communicative tools to more permanently rein in alphas. Their brief storms blow out without lasting effects. That would be less likely if they sometimes led to the death of, or serious injury to, the alpha. As we shall see, the early Pleistocene hominin situation was different in ways that would made resentment storms over attempts to monopolize the take much more dangerous. As with the chimps, early in this evolutionary trajectory, hominin resentment storms were probably intense but brief. But their angers and their resentments were weaponized, and hence much more dangerous. This suggests that attempts to monopolize the prize of collaboration were less likely, and less likely to be successful. As a consequence, there was often enough, an even-enough distribution of the profits of power scavenging to encourage this form of foraging, and to make it more central to hominin lifeways. A dominance-structured distribution would be set aside with some regularity for the distribution of a critical resource, making that form of immediate return mutualism resilient against cheating. Moreover, at least by the time erectines had become fairly regularly successful ambush hunters, they had, compared to the chimps, much superior capacities to control their impulses, understand their peers and coordinate with them. For ambush hunting depends on both coordination and impulse control. In Richard Gould's ethnography of Australian foragers of the Western Desert, he gives a vivid description of the discomforts of waiting motionless in wait for emus, in the heat, and being feasted upon by insects (Gould 1969).

Weapons matter. They make a collective eruption of anger likely to be lethal. As noted earlier, Paul Bingham took this to be the hominin-chimp difference-maker, giving teeth to a coalition of the weaker against the strong (Bingham 1999, Bingham 2000). His argument is essentially geometric. His idea was that weapons, even clubs, put some distance between attackers and target, so more can attack simultaneously. There is more room in the front row, and the increased weight of fire is decisive, as is the increased division of risk, as the size of the enforcement coalition increases. There is something to this idea (though it applies more cleanly to ambush hunting), but it understates the agency of the target. In my view, the more important factor is that weapons put single shot lethality on the table, and that they make spontaneous bursts of anger seriously risky for their target, even if those impulses only last a few seconds. Arms elevate risk. Consider, for example, a large subadult male hominin encountering a party of three or four females returning to camp with some prized food (honey, or eggs).[6] The male is likely to be much stronger than any single female, and a group of three or four could do very little if he knocked one down and helped himself. Would the threat of being punched or kicked seriously deter such bullying? Now suppose they are armed with digging sticks. I have a traditional Australian Aboriginal digging stick, and in effect it is a short wooden spear: about a meter long, made of hard wood, weighing about 2 kg, sharpened at each end. Underground Storage Organs are often quite deep, in hard ground. A digging stick needs to have substantial weight and strength for leverage, and the sharper the better. It needs heft. With such a tool, a woman behind or beside our bully is a real threat, if she has the will to use it. A full-bodied thrust will inflict a serious wound, and late Pliocene medical services were probably not ideal. Weaponized aggressive encounters just are inherently more risky. They raise the stakes, even when one or both sides are probably bluffing. Anger, fear, frustration

---

[6] Of course, until respect for possession is habitual, however hungry their children and grandchildren might be, they would be well-advised to eat such treats before heading back with whatever lesser finds they had.

and weapons can turn a minor squabble into a serious injury, or worse. Moreover, early Pleistocene hominins were probably less in control of their eruptive emotions than were later ones. Even in Anatomically Modern Human forager societies, murder rates from spontaneous outbreaks of anger are quite high (Boehm 2000).

While weapons by themselves are a difference-maker, to suppress dominance they need to be linked to enduring motivation and an ability to act together. Anger and resentment of bullying and free-riding were unlikely to be in short supply. So this picture envisages that the suppression of dominance was initially irruptive, partial and temporary.[7] Very likely making it more complete and more sustained was a slow and incremental process. It was conditional on improved capacities to communicate and coordinate, and improved impulse control. On this analysis, over evolutionary time the motivation to suppress bullying shifted from flares of hot but brief reactive attitudes to become more sustained and persisting. Erectines or Heidelbergensians learned to treasure and sustain their resentments, a psychology not wholly unknown in AMHs. Collective hunting and power scavenging select for coordination and impulse control, so once any form of sharing pirated kills through immediate return mutualism established in the hominin lineage, selection for foraging efficiencies builds the social and cognitive capacities that can make the suppression of bullies more complete and lasting. Better executive capacities make sustained plans more likely to be executed, less likely to misfire through distraction, temptation and memory failure. These capacities allow a temporary coalition powered by hot emotions to gradually transition into a more stable coalition with more enduring motivations. Forager egalitarianism may well have been fully and stably established only

---

[7] Does this scenario face a "second order" free-rider problem? Would a timid or less reactive bandmember who hung back from a resentment explosion be advantaged? Perhaps. That depends on (i) the risk of being part of a collective attack; (ii) whether those who suppressed the bully also helped themselves to more of the spoils, just by being closer; (iii) whether the timid suffered a reputational penalty.

with the emergence of the Heidelbergensians.[8] Even so, if Bunn and Pickering are right, these capacities were emerging in early erectine populations as they became competent ambush hunters. The gene-culture coevolution of the physical, cognitive, emotional, technical, informational and social capacities that made cooperation in foraging *profitable* also provided important elements in the repertoire that made cooperation *stable*, including weapons and the will and organizational capacity to use them to limit cheating.

The scenario just developed makes it possible to explain how early hominin forager bands—bands of erectus hominins—cooperated successfully and stably, though probably in limited ways, without language, norms, or other complex cognitive or cultural tools. The social scale of cooperation matters. Even at the scale of forager bands (perhaps averaging 15 or so adults) contingent cooperation—I will cooperate if and only if others do—is not stable. For if I withdraw cooperation in response to an episode of cheating, I impact not just on the cheat but on those still cooperating, reducing further their incentive to keep cooperating. Robert Boyd, Pete Richerson and Joseph Henrich (with various co-authors) have pointed out that for risky or expensive forms of cooperation to be stable, deterring cheating had to be collective, not individual (Boyd and Richerson 2001, Boyd, Gintis et al. 2005, Boyd 2016, Henrich 2016). The band as a whole, or most of it, had to reward cooperation and punish cheats. In almost all cases, it will be too risky for a single individual to do so. So they argue that band-scale cooperation requires some extra mechanism that mobilizes the band; one that identifies cheating as cheating and motivates a deterring response. They suggest that explicit norms play this role.[9] Such norms

---

[8] In recent work, Richard Wrangham has suggested an even later date, around the time of the emergence of AMHs (Wrangham 2018). But that view struggles to accommodate the evidence of a long history of Pleistocene cooperation.

[9] Norms need not be explicit. Contemporary social life is shaped by many implicit norms about, for example, social distance and conversational turn-taking. But Boyd's discussion of Turkana cooperation and the role of norms in controlling free-riding depends on the norms being explicit ((Boyd 2016) pp 87–91).

make cheating unambiguous, and motivate and shape a punishing response. There is indeed evidence that many contemporary humans are moralizing punishers, being willing to pay some cost to inflict a harm on a cheat, even if that cheat has made no difference to their own situation (Gächter, Herrmann et al. 2010). If that is right, it makes the role of culture in stabilizing cooperation important early in the evolution of hominin cooperation. For early Pleistocene hunting is evidence of band-level cooperation, and the distinctive norms of a group are built and transmitted by cultural learning, often with considerable community investment in making those norms stick. On this picture, only the cultural transmission of norms would make band-scale cooperation in hunting and other activities stable.

In my view, this line of argument overstates the cultural and cognitive capacities needed for the simplest forms of immediate return mutualism. First, this line of thought overlooks a crucial distinction between cooperation based on reciprocation and cooperation taking the form of immediate return mutualism. If Thag is stiffed by Thrug through Thrug's failure to reciprocate Thag's help, Thag must either impose costs on Thrug himself, which may be too risky, or elicit help. He needs to attract third party support: support from those aware of Thrug's actions, but not directly affected by those actions. That is why norms matter; Thag must show that Thrug acted wrongly. But if in the context of collective action, Thrug had attempted to pirate most of a kill (or has obviously failed to do his share of securing it), all of the group, Thag and all the others, are directly and adversely impacted. If Thag is the first to object, he needs support, but not *third party* support. When faced by egregious cheating, everyone else stands to lose and lose seriously, and this is common knowledge. That is why relatively simple cognitive and motivational mechanisms suffice to deter bullying and free-riding in mutualist cooperation. Collective resentment at being sponged upon or ripped off deters cheating on a scale that would destabilize cooperation. All that is required is that these hominins would resent any attempt to secure a share obviously larger than their own. Given that, band-scale cooperation can be stabilized by the hot emotions of frustrated expectation, resenting the loss of an anticipated gain and the spread of that anger though a group already highly aroused through making a kill or seizing a kill.

There is every reason to believe ancestral hominins would resent such pirating. For there is a discussion in the primate literature of "inequality aversion," with entertaining experiments showing capuchins' resentment of another monkey getting grapes while the focal monkey gets monkey chow (Brosnan and de Waal 2003). One might be tempted to think of this as itself evidence of protonormative thinking. But "inequality aversion," is a misleading name for the phenomenon: monkeys do not mind getting more than others; they just resent getting less. That is all that is needed, motivationally, to fuel collective responses to attempts to pirate or monopolize the profits of cooperation.

So band-level cooperation that takes the form of collective action with immediate returns can establish and stabilise even though the cooperating agents are not motivated by social norms that they have internalised. That is fortunate for the analysis of cooperation, for some forms of cooperation must precede the emergence of social worlds regulated by explicit social norms. Explicit norms require language, or something close to language, and other features of contemporary minds. Yet the cognitive and social resources needed to transmit, accept and be guided by norms could only evolve in an environment with a fair degree of long-sustained cooperation. Early hominin co-operators could not have language or anything that approximates language, for language is itself a cognitively and socially complex form of cooperation. It depends on a very sophisticated set of cognitive capacities; capacities that are selected only in a social world that is already cooperative. While cooperation and communication no doubt coevolve, with enhanced communication making new forms of cooperation possible, the first steps in band-scale cooperation could not have required the sophistication of a social life guided by explicit norms, with all the communicative sophistication that implies.

In short: In my view we have a plausible, though still speculative conception of the suppression of dominance hierarchy and the establishment of mutualist collective action in the hominin lineage; a suppression that was probably partial and unstable until quite deep into the Pleistocene. However, cooperation based on reciprocation, especially indirect reciprocation, requires a larger social and cognitive toolkit. In part, that is for the reason we have just seen: cooperation that takes the form of networks of reciprocation probably does depend on third party support in sanctioning cooperation failures, and that is more challenging cognitively and motivationally. As we shall now see, it requires a good deal of communicative sophistication as well.

2.3 An Economy of Reciprocation

In 1.1, I confessed that the analysis of this essay depended on three controversial claims about hominin history. One of those claims becomes important here: in my view, late in the Pleistocene indirect reciprocation became increasingly important in forager life. Here, the distinction between direct and indirect reciprocation is important. Indirect reciprocation is a form of cooperation in which a focal agent makes a contribution to the welfare of others, with that contribution being rewarded later, but not necessarily by those he/she aided. Direct reciprocation involves the exchange of help: you help me now; I help you later. While I shall argue that indirect reciprocation became important only in the late Pleistocene, direct reciprocation very likely played some role in the lives of erectine and Heidelbergensian foragers, and perhaps an important one. If ethnographic data is any guide to early Pleistocene success rates, hunts failed more often, perhaps much more often, than they succeeded. That is especially important if a single hunt required the participation of all or most of the adults (or the adult males) of a band. It probably did, for in hunting large animals with low velocity wooden spears, once an ambush was sprung, weight of fire would be needed to bring the target down reasonably quickly. If a hunt fails, then a large part of the band will be empty-handed. If hunting has a low success rate, some back-up food source is essential; food that can be found reliably, even if it is less appealing. In ethnographically known foragers of the tropics, subtropics and warm temperate environments, women provided that back-up from gathered resources: small game and plants. Reciprocation is fundamental to these economies: males are fed gathered resources from their partner (and/or other members of their fairly immediate family). Successful hunts end up with meat being shared fairly widely in the band.[10] Gathered foods tend to be shared more narrowly within the family, perhaps because gathering success is less dependent on luck and more on effort. So hunting is made viable only by a gendered division of labour and reciprocal flows of food in the band.

Does the evidence of erectine and Heidelbergensian hunting show that something like this gendered division of labour has a deep history, and hence that reciprocation, likewise, has a deep history? Perhaps there was something like an early gendered division of labour, where the males as a group provided meat when they were collectively successful, in return for gathered foods, but there are two other possibilities. (i) Resource availability is often highly seasonal. So perhaps early hunters hunted only in the boom seasons, when fall-back resources could be quickly and readily

---

[10] There is some controversy about the extent to which a successful hunter can channel meat to his family and to other hunters who have treated him preferentially. This is important in the debate about whether male hunting is essentially family provisioning (hence breeding effort) or whether it is a display of fitness (hence mating effort). If early hunting was a collective activity of the males in the band as a whole, it is unlikely to be a display. In most cases, no individual would identifiably be the successful hunter, and there would be no audience to admire. For a sceptical view of the relationship between hunting and family provisioning, see (Hawkes 1991, Hawkes, O'Connell et al. 2010, Hawkes, O'Connell et al. 2018). For a defence of the importance of that relationship, see (Gurven and Hill 2006, Gurven and Hill 2009, Gurven and Hill 2010).

gathered. (ii) Perhaps early hunters were more reliably successful than ethnographically known hunters. Of these two alternatives, the first seems more likely: early in this evolutionary history, hunters hunted only when fallback resources were readily available. It is possible, though, that early hunters were more reliably successful: perhaps early Pleistocene ungulates were naive about the threat hominins posed; perhaps there were far more targets in a world without farms and farmers. It is also possible that a division of labour was based (say) on age rather than gender, with subadults gathering fallback resources. So hunting does not *necessarily* imply a gendered division of labour. Even so, it is possible that there was some form of reciprocation between the genders, presumably mediated by sex and reproduction, fairly early in hominin foraging economies. This would place the origins of some form of pair-bonding early (as argued by (Chapais 2008)). If indeed it was early, it involved a form of direct reciprocation that is intrinsically quite stable. The time horizons are very short; interaction is very regular between mated partners; they have common genetic interests in their children, and hence in each others' continued health. Other forms of reproductive cooperation could also be stabilized by direct reciprocation: turn-about child minding would allow mothers to forage unencumbered by toddlers. This would be a form of low cost, high value, symmetrical and regular reciprocation. It is readily stabilized by a contingent willingness to cooperate as long as the favour was returned.

So while we do not know its exact character, it is likely that some form of direct reciprocal cooperation was a feature of erectine and/or Heidelbergensian social life. I shall suggest that a late Pleistocene reboot of the hominin foraging economy changed the relative importance of reciprocation and immediate return mutualism, with indirect reciprocation becoming important. This change in the relative importance of reciprocation and mutualism was gradual, unstable and not coordinated over space. This picture of a gradually emerging new Pleistocene economy is based on two new aspects of late Pleistocene lifeways: an expansion of their resource envelop, and the emergence of projectile weapons. First, between about 120 kya and 50 kya, there was a very significant expansion in the resources harvested, especially with a much more systematic exploitation of seashore and riverine resources (Marean 2011), and more intense exploitation of plants (with grindstones beginning to appear in the record). Prior to this period, foragers were hunters and gatherers: fish and allied resources did not seem to play much role in their economy (and while fish bones might not preserve, shellfish middens would (Marean, Bar-Matthews et al. 2007), (Klein and Steele 2013)).

In the second half of this period, the projectile revolution arrived, perhaps beginning about 100 kya[11] (O'Driscoll and Thompson 2018). Some foragers began to use the javelin plus woomera, or the bow and arrow, though, as often with a technical innovation, the initial record is patchy and ambiguous. Projectile technology may have been lost or abandoned at times, too. But once it established it was very important. Hunting with high velocity weapons changes the shape of hunting, for it favours individual or small parties aiming to stalk or ambush. Numbers at the kill are no longer crucial, and a single hunter or a pair have a much better chance of a concealed stalk or ambush than a larger group. Moreover, the band as a whole will cover the local area more efficiently. Collectively, the expansion of the resource portfolio and the projectile revolution encourages a shift from larger to smaller foraging parties. Different resources—shellfish; a nesting colony of birds; different species of game—are found in different places, and so are more efficiently harvested by the band dispersing in pursuit of their separate targets.

In sum, these changes in foraging practice seem likely to make a band's foraging collectively more efficient. Broadening the

---

[11] Detecting this technology is not easy. It relies on the ethnographic evidence that the points of stabbing spears are typically heavier and more robust than javelin and arrow points. Impact scars can help too. But these are only tendencies.

resource base might have some costs, if and as it includes targeting resources with a lower rate of return per unit of effort. But it will buffer the band against failure. The greater the resource portfolio, the less likely it is that all sources of supply will fail at once. All else equal, the flow of resources will be more resilient. Most obviously, space is searched more efficiently if a number of small parties try their luck in different spots, rather than staking the whole day on a few possibilities. A shift to small hunting parties and to a broader foraging spectrum, supported by appropriate expertise and equipment, would significantly enhance the profits of cooperation. The total take goes up, and risk is managed more effectively. However, cooperation sustained by direct and indirect reciprocation is significantly harder to monitor and police than immediate return mutualism. Here is why.

First: the shift to small hunting parties will have an unmasking effect. For each party, success will be variable, and if ethnology is our guide, failure will be more common than success. Luck is important, influencing which animals are encountered, and in what circumstances. But skill and drive will play a role too, and it is hardly possible that these will be uniform across the band's hunters. Differences in ability that were somewhat masked when the band hunted as a group will now be on display, if and as different parties have markedly different success rates. There is a serious risk of social tension: treat the less successful differentially and they will resent it; treat them equally, and risk resentment as the more competent support the less competent.

Second: with immediate return mutualism the challenge of resource commensurability is relatively minor. If a group of fishers cooperate in setting and then dragging in a net full of fish, it is relatively easy to assess a proposed division of the take. True: fish come in different sizes and some species are more desirable than others. But recognizing a roughly equal distribution is fairly easy, and the same is true of a division of a kill, even though portions of an animal are not all of the same value. As the resource portfolio expands, so does the problem of commensurability. You return to camp with a bag of mussels. How much of a duck tomorrow is your contribution of mussels worth? Even the fair-minded could disagree about that. Moreover, context and time complicate commensurability still further. Suppose you were the only forager to succeed that day: everyone else would go hungry but for your mussels, and you did go somewhat hungry because there were so many wanting to share. Does that mean you can expect a whole duck tomorrow? Should you expect more, and how much more, if it is a couple of weeks before reciprocation comes your way? This problem might be eased if only large resource parcels are shared outside the immediate family (and this seems to be a pattern amongst some foragers).[12]

Third, the problems of commensurability and temporal displacement between contribution and return make it more difficult for a focal agent to assess the flow of benefit amongst other agents. If the spoils of collective action are distributed on the spot, it will soon become obvious if someone is always angling for more. Persistent greed will be clear to the affected parties. That is much less true in systems of indirect reciprocation. Individuals and small parties return to camp at different times. If they share with others, or benefit from others sharing with them, those transactions will often be over before others make it home. Band members do not have direct, observational knowledge of the contribution histories of others. So tracking cheating no longer depends on public information that

---

[12] Joeri Witteveen suggests an alternative: resource incommensurability opens up a role for a proto-market mechanism, especially if the availability of different resources fluctuates markedly (for then a fixed norm of appropriate exchange is unlikely to be stable). He discusses the ethnographic work of Adrian Jaeggi on the Tsiname, who exchange resources in a market-like but restricted way: specific material goods for specific material goods; specific services for specific services. Witteveen's point about the interaction between resource incommensurability and fluctuations in supply is well-taken, but a proto-market can at most mediate or substitute for direct reciprocation, and not even that if one resource is directly bartered for another. In a direct trade, there is no first mover disadvantage, as there is with reciprocation, and that makes barter less vulnerable to cheating. In reciprocation-based cooperation, those who give help first are vulnerable to failures of return. But for the same reason, reciprocation manages risk over time, in ways barter may not.

flows from being part of a cooperative interaction. Of course, band-level societies are remarkably informationally transparent, and all the members of a band know who is generous and who is stingy. But in part this depends on a culturally evolved tool: gossip. Gossip is not needed to monitor greed and free-riding in collective action mutualisms, and nor is it needed in systems of direct reciprocation, where agents help particular individuals who in turn are expected to return that help. Direct reciprocation relies on memory and an appropriate assessment of favours given and returned to ensure mutual fairness. But it does not need gossip. Indirect reciprocation does. Gossip does not solve the problem of settling on a local consensus on what counts as a fair contribution, but once a consensus establishes, it is probably essential for tracking fair dealing in systems of indirect reciprocation. That matters, for indirect reciprocation is the form of cooperation needed to manage risk. All parties in the band chase resources, but with variable success. Your contribution today is matched by *whoever* happens to be successful tomorrow.

In some forager societies, cooperation over food takes the form of "demand sharing": anyone who has food is obliged to share it with those who have none, on request (Marlowe 2010, Lewis 2015). In practice, demand sharing is probably a mix of indirect reciprocation with some free-riding. That free-riding is tolerated because the social friction costs of excluding the somewhat slack outweigh the benefits of doing so, and perhaps, as Nicolas Peterson suggests, because the effort of accurate booking keeping is not worth its costs (Peterson 1993). While demand sharing opens the door to free-riding, its effect is limited by informal pressures to be productive and by hiding the most desirable items from view or eating them before returning to camp (Peterson 1993, Marlowe 2010). Cooperative habits can persist despite modest levels of free-riding; it is less of a threat than bullying.

Fourth, picking up on the point made at the end of 2.2, when cheating occurs in mutualistic interactions—someone is slack or greedy—the interests of the others are affected in broadly similar ways. It is in all their interests to deter such behaviour. Interests are aligned. That need not be true of networks of reciprocation. Suppose again that I have brought mussels regularly back to camp and rightly come to think that I have been ungenerously treated. Return favours are rarer and stingier than I expect. I face two problems. First, this may be my problem alone. Others might take themselves to be treated reasonably. If there is retaliation to be done, to deter future stinginess, I have to do it myself, bearing all the costs and risks myself. Second, who should I retaliate against? When reciprocity is direct, an agent who is short-changed knows who is to blame, and can respond accordingly. When reciprocity is indirect, it is less obvious who should have been more generous and when. Everyone's general responsibility is no-one's specific responsibility. In real forager communities, someone who feels badly dealt with will complain long, loud and normally to some effect. Ethnography documents plenty of complaining about lack of generosity (Marlowe 2010, Boehm 2012, Wiessner 2014, Lewis 2015). However, we need to explain why complaining so often *works*. Why do others care about accusations of stinginess? As with gossip, we see here a culturally evolved mechanism that helps stabilize cooperation. Norms of generosity matter in such societies, and those living in them are sensitive to claims that they have failed to be generous.

Fifth, the shift towards reciprocation and broader-spectrum foraging has indirect effects that stress the social contract. For an increase in resource breadth makes mobility decisions more difficult, as resources exhaust at different rates, and because it is worth harvesting less valuable resources only if they are close to the campsite. In thinking about the economics of forager mobility, Lewis Binford distinguished between two modes of mobility (Binford 1980). Residentially mobile foragers move their base regularly, and forage by day trips from that base. Logistically mobile foragers move their base camp less regularly, but task groups leave for days or weeks, sleeping at a bivouac, targeting a particular resource, harvesting, processing, returning to camp. Logistic mobility is one response to the problem of the differential rates at which resources deplete, so for some of the foragers it is time to move, but not yet for others. Likewise, it is a response to a boom in a specific resource at a predictable location, but one that is otherwise not very productive (like a seabird breeding colony on an offshore island). But it imposes stress on social life. Social cohesion can no longer be managed by daily, face-to-face interactions. Moreover, it can create uncertainty about sexual fidelity. For some are away for days or weeks, while others remain.

The upshot of this section is that foragers who share through indirect reciprocation gather resources more efficiently, and manage risk more effectively, than those who cooperate only through direct exchange and mutualistic collective action. But cooperation that depends on indirect reciprocation is prone to conflict, and so it depends on a much more elaborate set of cultural tools. These include gossip, norms and ritual.

2.4 Making Reciprocation Work: Gossip

Erectine and Heidelbergensian foragers must have had considerable communicative capacities: probably some form of "protolanguage." This is a hypothetical, cut-down form of language, with nouns, verbs and modifiers, but with little or no overt syntax or morphology: no tense markers; no case markers; no regular pluralization; no way of forming subordinate structures like that-clauses. The idea is based on pidgins and trade lingua franca: systems that emerge amongst adult agents who have no language in common (Jackendoff 1999, Bickerton 2002). They are often effective tools, but over a restricted range of topics, like trading interactions, and they are heavily dependent on context and mutual knowledge. In some cases these systems do not even have fixed word order to indicate agent and patient. Arguably, a system like this is all that erectines and Heidelbergensians would have needed. It would be enough to organize collaboration in foraging and to support intergenerational learning, by supplying verbal labels for the kinds juveniles needed to recognize and distinguish. There was probably a restricted range of issues about which communication was important, and shared background knowledge would have been extensive (this view is developed in detail in Planer and Sterelny forthcoming).

As we have seen, late Pleistocene humans needed more. Systems of reciprocation are stable only if reputation is reliable. In a social environment in which interaction is dispersed in space and time between small parties and individuals, reliable reputation depends on gossip: on reports of these interactions. Others are your eyes and ears only if they are able to tell you what they have seen and heard.[13] In turn, gossip is linguistically demanding: the gossip needs to be able to specify who did what to whom, when and where, and with some precision. And perhaps *why*: motivation matters in gossip. Furthermore, what others do includes what others say: so gossip needs mechanisms of reporting speech. Moreover, as the community is more dispersed, the exchange of gossip can rely less on common knowledge. The information gradient is steeper in more dispersed communities: there is less informational overlap from individual to individual. That makes language both more useful and also more demanding, as more must be explicit in the utterance itself. Any substantial shift to reciprocation would have needed a language upgrade, and as we shall see, not just for gossip, and for more complex coordination and negotiation. For explicit norms are important in maintaining indirect reciprocation, and these must be articulated, explained and defended. Late Pleistocene foragers needed to talk about what should happen, and why it should

---

[13] Robin Dunbar has also argued that selection for the capacity to gossip drove the evolution of language, but for rather different reasons (Dunbar 1996).

happen, not just what did happen. Narrative was probably important by this stage in hominin evolution, too. It is a universal feature of human social life (Boyd 2009), and is often a vehicle for encoding community norms (Smith, Schlaepfer et al. 2017), and as part of the ritual life of the community. So late Pleistocene foragers probably had the linguistic skills to express and understand explicitly fictional and esoteric narratives.

It is one thing to have the linguistic tools to gossip about your social partners; another, for that possibility to influence their social behaviour. Why do foragers care about gossip? What makes their reputations matter to them? The literature on wealth distinguishes three forms of wealth: material capital, embodied capital and social capital (Bowles, Smith et al. 2010). Mobile foragers do not have much material capital, because they are mobile. They have to carry their goods with them, or cache them safely, when they move to a new camp, and this constrains how much they can accumulate. Embodied capital is the sum of an agent's physical and cognitive skills together with their health, strength and endurance. Social capital sums the social support an agent can expect as he/she faces the trials of life. These include support in conflicts, and support when sick or injured. In addition, social capital influences the options an agent has to shift to a new band if the local patch becomes inhospitable (for instance, if there is a locust plague, or some other local disaster). It is relevant to an agent's prospects of negotiating a good marriage for self or relatives. San and Hadza parents want their daughters to marry reliable and supportive hunters, and so a would-be son-in-law needs to be of good repute. In short, both embodied and social capital are central to a forager's life prospects (Smith, Hill et al. 2010). Reputation is obviously critical to social capital, but it matters as well to embodied capital, as it influences access to information and hence one's skill set. In particular, in some forager cultures access to ritual knowledge is quite tightly controlled, and being fully initiated into the group matters. Having the right to secret knowledge is itself an important form of social capital (Keen 2006). It follows that foragers have very good reason to care about reputation. So one of the mechanisms which makes reciprocation work in these societies is the possession of language, or at least a rich enough proto-language to support gossip. The practice of gossip enables information (and sometimes misinformation) about one's bandmates to circulate freely through the group, from multiple sources, and that circulation makes information that only a few know first-hand common knowledge. Agents respond because reputation matters; agents care about what others think of them.

Reliable reputation allows co-operators to associate with others who also cooperate. That matters, for an important general principle has emerged from theoretical work on cooperation. The stability of cooperation is always under threat if in interactions between co-operators and defectors, defectors do better. That is likely when cooperative acts have costs, as sharing one's resources does. For costly cooperation to be stable, birds of a feather must flock together: co-operators must mostly interact with other co-operators. If co-operators do indeed predominantly associate with one another, the fact that co-operator/co-operator interactions go well for both swamps the cost to co-operators of the occasional cheating defector. These are left to harvest the miserable returns of their own grudging interactions. Reputation leverages the preferential association of co-operators with each other.

This mechanism does not depend on gossip being perfectly accurate. But it does depend on it being quite reliable. In intimate environments in which everyone regularly interacts with everyone, that supposition is realistic. In a multi-sender, multi-receiver network, the risks of both deception and mere error are lowered, as receivers typically have access to independent channels through which information flows about salient incidents. This access to alternative witnesses limits the effect of error and deceit. Both are more of a threat in private than public talk.

2.5 Making Reciprocation Work: Norms

Gossip was not the only mechanism that mattered. In 2.2, I denied the claim that the emergence of normatively guided social lives was critical to *any* band-level cooperation. While I agreed that the costs of enforcing cooperation need to be spread across the whole cooperating party, I rejected the view that only accepted and internalized norms could motivate collective response to cooperation failure. But while mutualist cooperation does not depend on the evolution of accepted, endorsed and internalized public norms, those norms probably were important for the late Pleistocene economy of reciprocation.

In those economies, norms play two important roles.

One is the reduction of ambiguity. In 2.3, I pointed out that one of the challenges of indirect reciprocation is uncertainty, especially as the resource portfolio expands. How much should an agent expect to share? What are others' legitimate expectations of him/her? What are the agent's reasonable expectations of others? If those expectations are not met, who is to blame? These risks of disagreement and conflict go up:

(i) as more individuals are involved;
(ii) as individual relationships become more complex, with agents having multiple and perhaps conflicting obligations;
(iii) as there are more kinds of goods and services in circulation through sharing and reciprocation (rather than direct exchange);
(iv) as the temporal scale over which agents need to track their own and others' contribution history goes up;
(v) as role differentiation increases, with different agents consistently contributing (or failing to contribute) in distinct ways to the welfare of the group;
(vi) as the spatial scale of social life increases. For, despite gossip, increases in scale inevitably lead to less certainty about what others have done.

These factors all make it more probable that agents will misunderstand one another's expectations; for there to be errors of observation and memory; for there to be strongly divergent views about relative value. A band of saints could disagree vigorously in these circumstances. Pleistocene forager bands were not composed of saints, and so the objective potentials for conflict would have been exacerbated by individuals' natural biases in finding their own contributions more salient than those of others. Norms that *explicitly specify* the obligations to share, and the expectations each agent has of others (for example, expectations about the obligations of sons and daughters to support their parents-in-law) reduce this uncertainty, and hence reduce conflict flash-points. There is plenty of evidence that many historically known foragers had explicit norms of distribution, sometimes very elaborate ones. For example, in Gould's ethnography of West Desert Aboriginal Australians, he details the norms that determine the distribution of meat from a successful kangaroo hunt ((Gould 1969) pp 16–17). Named portions of the roo go to specific classes of the hunter's relatives (everyone is some relative or other), and that portion is then divided within the class (for example, the father-in-law's brothers might get one shoulder to share). Those entitled to share need not be involved in the hunt itself. Division rules make explicit what is expected in an impersonal way: all kangaroos caught are divided by the same rules. In reducing uncertainty, such norms damp down conflict points and reduce transaction costs. Even without conflict, if every episode of sharing and reciprocation had to be negotiated from scratch, it would be a time-consuming and wearing process, like shopping in a market without fixed prices.

What explains the content of these varying sharing norms? That is not known, but I assume it is some mix of (i) historical contingency, (ii) the pre-existing emotional and cognitive dispositions of the humans in question; (iii) incentivizing continued cooperation given the local ecology. Norms of sharing are most unlikely to exactly match a typical agent's contributions and receipts, but wildly discrepant ones would not be stable; and (iv) structural differences within communities. For example, norms in Australian Aboriginal communities seem biased in favour of older men (see, for example, (Hart and Pilling 1960)). These structural differences become particularly important as the normative and ritual landscape changes with the emergence of inegalitarian societies, as we shall see in 4.3.

There is another important and influential suggestion about the factors that explain social norms. The thought is that cultural group selection plays an essential role in explaining their character. This idea is based on an empirical claim coupled to modelling work. The models show that many systems of norms are stable once established. Indeed, these models show that once established, even viciously anti-social, maladaptive norms can persist, because they are stabilized by punishment. The formal work indicated that normatively regulated communities have many possible equilibrium points. Yet, the claim goes, in most societies norms mostly enforce prosocial behaviour (Curry, Mullins et al. 2019). Their candidate explanation: communities that happen to equilibrate on prosocial norms tend to out-compete those that do not (Boyd and Richerson 1992, Henrich 2006). I return to the role of community-level selection in the explanation of cooperation in 3.4. But I do not think it is surprising that prosocial norms are moderately common. We do not need community-level selection to explain this. While punishment can stabilize just about any norm once it becomes accepted and enforced in a community, to establish a candidate norm must resonate with the pre-existing cognitive and emotional dispositions of these ancient humans. As Shaun Nicholls has pointed out, living humans have capacities for empathy and sympathy that make prosocial norms salient and appealing (Nichols 2004). The argument of this chapter suggests that norms became important relatively recently in our evolutionary history. If so, the minds of the first norm-abiding humans were likely to resemble modern humans in this respect, as their minds have already been shaped by a long history of association and collaboration, resulting in stronger and more vivid social emotions. So they too will be apt to find candidate prosocial norms more credible and appealing.

On this analysis then, while there will be lots of normative variation between communities, in most communities, most social norms will endorse somewhat prosocial behaviour. In doing so, one of their main effects is the reduction of ambiguity about what to expect of yourself and others. The second role of norms is their relevance to third party motivation. By reducing ambiguity, norms of sharing and division make defecting more overt, less deniable. But it is one thing to detect cheating, another to respond to it. As noted earlier, one important difference between reciprocation and mutualism is that the costs of reciprocation failure can easily fall on a single individual, and, often, that individual alone could not afford the costs of sanctioning the cheat. He or she needs third party support. Yet what will move those third parties to intervene? It is true that third parties may have some stake in the sanction, even when they are not personally affected by this particular defection. Someone who has successfully cheated once may well be encouraged to cheat again, perhaps at the onlooker's expense. Even so, it is likely that internalized norms, and the outrage that flagrant violations then provoke, are essential in mobilizing third party support to sanction cheating. Experimental evidence from behavioural economics shows that some third parties (but not all) will pay a cost to inflict punishment on grossly unfair offers in ultimatum games, and to punish agents who fail to contribute to a common pool in public goods games (Gächter, Herrmann et al. 2010). These experiments are designed to exclude instrumental punishment: the onlookers who punish have no reason to believe they will interact in the future with the defector. Norms can motivate rewards and sanctions, and individuals in mobile forager societies genuinely endorse, and deeply internalize, norms of sharing (Boehm 1999, Boehm 2012). That is why complaints of stinginess are loudly made, and it is why they are effective.

In sum: I am sceptical of the Boyd-Richerson-Henrich view that norms are essential in explaining any costly band-level cooperation. But I think they are right when the stability of cooperation depends on third party support in deterring defection. That support often depends on the fact that third parties recognize that a norm has been violated, and that they care. However, the appeal to norms poses an obvious challenge. How could human psychology have evolved the capacity to notice, internalize and act on norms, if those actions involve costs when your own interests are not at stake? How could selection have favoured the evolution of a motivational system that would prompt agents to engage in costly, disinterested punishment? This challenge requires a two-part answer. Why did selection favour a mind that internalized norms? What was the incremental pathway from a mind innocent of norms to one that internalizes them? The selective challenge is answered by returning to the central role of reputation in forager society. On average an agent is fitter (probably much fitter) if he or she is regarded by peers as reliable, trustworthy and fair rather than selfish or unreliable. Yet, as Robert Frank cogently argued in *Passion within Reason*, by far the most convincing way of seeming trustworthy is to actually be trustworthy (Frank 1988). That is especially true in small social worlds where it is hard to keep secrets and conceal failures. Internalizing the norms of the culture is selectively favoured as an investment in good reputation. Occasionally it will have costs, but for the most part an agent with that reputation will reap the rewards of trust.

Jonathan Birch has suggested a promising though speculative answer to the second question (Birch forthcoming). His idea is that normative guidance is a form of skilled action, and it evolved first in the context of skilled craftsmanship. The road to norms begins with pride (or with discontent, if something has gone wrong) in craftsmanship; caring about your work, perhaps partly for instrumental reasons, but importantly for intrinsic reasons as well. Skilled craftsmen hold themselves to a standard of achievement, and are dissatisfied with a product below that standard, whether or not anyone else knows or cares. Likewise, those agents find successful, skilled execution intrinsically as well as instrumentally rewarding. Such intrinsic motivations are likely to have material rewards, motivating the practice and care that lead to mastery. This suggestion locates the initial origins of norms in the Acheulian, for some handaxes are beautifully made. As Birch points out, once normative guidance of craft skills establishes, we can expect individual standards of appropriate execution to converge; for them to become shared by social learning, teaching and mutual observation. None of this requires language: these standards can be shared but implicit. For forager artisans tend to work communally in a public space (Stout 2002, Hiscock 2014). That is especially true if artisans work together on a single tool, for then they must coordinate on a shared aim, and there is suggestive evidence of collective tool-making as far back as the Acheulian (Shipton 2010). On this picture, we expect norms of skilled work to become shared and then gradually become explicit in the local community. Pleistocene craftsmen developed intrinsic motivations to get it right or put it right, where getting it right included shared standards. Craft norms can become other-directed, if and to the extent that a skilled artisan feels discomfort, disapproval and/or the desire to intervene at the spectacle of another agent's inept workmanship. This might be one of the motivational foundations of teaching: intervening in response to the pain of seeing something done badly, not just through the desire to upskill the young.

To evolve social norms, we need a further incremental step to extend the scope of intrinsically motivated, standard-guided actions to social interaction, not just to physical crafts. A natural bridge here would be shared foraging activities, like hunting. These have elements of both craft skill and social interaction. There is a way of getting a hunt right, which has both social elements—smooth coordination, seamless division of the spoils—and precise physical execution. Pride in performance is the mother of normative guidance.

2.6 Making Reciprocation Work: Ritual

Acting on norms leaves no direct archaeological trace. But if ethnography is any guide, many of the norms of traditional cultures are transmitted with and through the ritual life of those communities. In turn, in these cultures, ritual is intimately connected to the material symbols of that community. Participants in rituals are painted; they wear masks and other paraphernalia (often elaborately decorated with feathers, shells and much else); their bodies are marked in various ways to indicate their ritual identity and role; there are totems, emblems and other special items of display. Some of these material symbols (feather headdresses, for example) would be archaeologically invisible. But some would be visible, if they were regularly used in Pleistocene ceremonies. Importantly, there is no sign of material symbols in the archaeological record of Heidelbergensians. But evidence of a ritual life begins to appear in the last 200 ky (Jaubert, Verheyden et al. 2016), and especially the last 100 ky (Rossano 2015).[14] The earliest is evidence of ochre use (though ochre can have utilitarian uses too). From a little over 100 kya, we see the first evidence of burials (at first, of Neanderthals (Pettitt 2011, Pettitt 2015)). We begin to find special places: places of sustained human action, but with no sign of domestic activity; no sign of food preparation or tool-making. The earliest so far seems to be a Neanderthal cave site at about 175 kya (Jaubert, Verheyden et al. 2016). The earliest jewellery is from about 100 kya; incised ochre at about 80 kya. The first musical instruments are dated at about 42 kya, but these bird-bone flutes are so musically sophisticated that they suggest a much deeper history of serious music making (Killin 2017).[15] Over this period, material symbols were

---

[14] There are a couple of older, but very controversial claims: a figurine from Morocco (dated to around 400 kya) and the so-called Venus of Berekhat Ram, from the Levant, an enigmatic, perhaps somewhat female-shaped pebble, that might be as old as 700 kya.

[15] Likewise, the earliest cave art, somewhat younger, is so sophisticated that it suggests a deeper artistic tradition.

becoming a more salient part of human material culture and this, in connection with the evidence of burials and special places, suggests that ritual was becoming a more important part of human life.

Ritual and religion are intimately associated, and I will take up the evolutionary emergence of religion in a little more detail in 4.3.[16] I shall argue there that changes in the character of ritual and religion played a significant role in mediating the emergence of less equal communities. In mobile forager social life, ritual, and the esoteric narratives associated with ritual, are in part vehicles for the transmission of norms. But they also play an experiential role, and in doing so they increase group cohesion and hence reduce the fragmenting effects of conflict and disagreement (Lewis 2013, Lewis 2016). So while ritual and religion are relevant to the stability of an economy of reciprocation through their role of transmitting norms and giving them authority, ritual is also relevant to the stability of these forager economies through their experiential effects. I have argued that an economy of reciprocation imposes real stresses on cohesion, and so I suggest that proto-religion emerged (or expanded in its social significance) in part as a response to these stresses. The performative aspects of these proto-religions were important for their powerful and bonding experiential effects. On this hypothesis, proto-religion consisted in multimodal performances of music, ritual and dance, often combined with experience-altering technologies. The experiential impacts of song, dance and performance were often supplemented and amplified by experience-altering drugs or by stressing the cognitive system in other ways: sleep deprivation, extremes of heat or cold (for example, Native American sweat lodges), sensory overload, exhaustion or just through the intensity of these emotionally charged events (Baumard and Boyer 2013). While mythic narratives play a central role in ethnographically documented small-world religious

---

[16] This account of religion and its evolution is further developed in (Sterelny 2017, Sterelny forthcoming-b).

traditions, these are often experienced as part of collective, socially bonding, socially marked, mixed modality performance, and often in the grip of altered states of consciousness. Agents encounter these narratives, which are often themselves far from mundane, as part of a package of intense and unusual perceptual experiences, and often while they are themselves taking an active part in the total performance, themselves engaged in coordinated, entrained song, ritual and dance.

On this view, the most ancient embodied proto-religions consisted in locally distinctive packages of collective ritual, ceremony, song and material symbolism. These packages sustained community affiliation and identity. As the social landscape became more complex, with inter-community relations becoming more important and perhaps more fraught, these experiential aspects of religion were supplemented through the addition of a characteristic set of mytho-poetic narratives: narratives that often asserted a community's identity, origin and connection to place.[17] Once inter-group relations had to balance the advantages of cooperation with the assertion of local rights, origin myths emphasizing that right to place were especially important. Flannery and Marcus emphasize the fact that one of the most pervasive norms of forager society is the right of first possession ((Flannery and Marcus 2012) chapter 4). This picture of the emergence and effect of early religion fits with known aspects of human psychology. Shared, synchronized activities bond participants. Collective, coordinated activity—singing and moving together in time—is known to have this bonding effect, reinforcing a sense of collective identity, especially when those affects are amplified by other mechanisms (music, for example, (McNeill 1997)). So too does a collective passage through intense, aversive, dangerous experience. Those who have survived combat together develop powerful mutual loyalty,

---

[17] Often mixed together with various recipes for intervention in a causally opaque world.

and the same is likely to be true of cohorts who have gone together through intense and terrifying rituals (Whitehouse and Lanman 2014, Whitehouse 2016).

In summary then, the late Pleistocene expansion of ritual is relevant to the argument of this chapter in two ways. Norms are often taught or reinforced though ritual, thus linking ritual life to the transmission of norms. One role of the mythic narratives associated with ritual is to explain and legitimize norms, often presented as coming from heroic quasi-human ancestors. So an increased presence of ritual suggests an increasing role for explicit norms. A second is that evidence of increased ritual activity is evidence of increased social stress, because ritual is a social mechanism that can ameliorate the effects of stress. So evidence of increased social investment in ritual is both a sign and a potential response to increased social tension. This is relevant as the shift to a more reciprocation-heavy form of cooperation is predicted to increase social tension, and hence we also expect to see in the record response to those increased tensions. While ritual has many roles in small scale societies, one of those roles is to reinforce group identity and solidarity (Whitehouse and Lanman 2014, Whitehouse 2016). In particular, initiation rituals can be seriously daunting. We do not know whether those of the Pleistocene were as terrifying, stressful and dangerous as some known from human ethnography. But if they were, those Pleistocene initiation classes would have experienced together dangerous, stressful, terrifying and painful experiences: collective experience analogous to those of combat. Harvey Whitehouse notes that many small world cultures include in their ritual repertoire rare but intense and aversive rituals, and he argues that these serve to bond individuals to support one another through dangerous and difficult times (Whitehouse and Lanman 2014, Whitehouse 2016). As I see it, the archaeological evidence of much greater investment in ritual activity from about 150 kya is evidence of communities under stress, with more internal tension as a result of changes in their foraging economy, and perhaps also from changes in band–band interactions. These communities managed those increased stresses in part through increased investment in actions that increased group cohesion and mutual loyalty.

2.7 Stabilizing Cooperation

In sum, the stability, not just the profitability, of Pleistocene cooperation depended on cultural tools: practices and skills that emerged gradually, piecemeal, and were then transmitted by cultural inheritance from one generation to the next: language rich enough to make gossip easy and detailed; explicit norms that specified individual obligations and expectations in the production and distribution of resources (and of course much else); the emergence of material culture and a ritual life, a life that was both a vehicle for the transmission and acceptance of norms and a way of reinforcing local loyalty and social identity. Cooperative life was more stressed and conflict prone in the late Pleistocene, and so these cultural tools were more important then. Much else had to change with these changes in cooperation and culture. Human minds had to be able to use a much richer version of language, to understand and be moved by ritual and mythic narratives; see the world in terms not just of what has happened and will happen, but also in terms of what should and should not happen. The increasing scope of human cooperation depended on gene-culture coevolution: on the evolution of both cultural tools and the cognitive capacities to use them. In the next chapters we consider both the opportunities and the stresses imposed on human cooperative interaction by further changes in human life: greater social scale, and greater social complexity, especially the complexity of increasingly less equal worlds.

3
Cooperation in a Larger World

3.1 Cooperation between Bands

So far the main focus of analysis has been the hominin band: the party that camps overnight together, cooperating on a day-to-day basis in sharing food and other resources, in childcare, and in defence against predation (in those environments in which predators continued to be a threat). As we saw in 1.4 and 1.5, this overnight group is more or less the whole social world of a great ape. It is true that there is gene flow between great ape social groups, but that flow is primarily maintained by sub-adult dispersal. For example, a sub-adult female chimp will leave her natal group to join (with some difficulty and stress) an adjoining group. But sub-adult females are the only ones who can safely migrate, and once she has gone, she has gone. There are no return visits to check on mum, and to see how the siblings are getting on. In ethnographically-known forager societies, bands are not closed units. There is movement between them, both quasi-permanently and for visits short and long, by both genders and at many life stages. Moreover, social organization is vertically complex: bands are nested in communities, with size ranges between about 150 and 500 adults; and communities are part of ethnolinguistic groups, typically of a few thousand. Communities are an important aspect of forager social lives. Resource constraints can make it difficult for the whole community to assemble, but in many forager cultures there are seasons of relative plenty,[1] and

---

[1] Or for arid land foragers, times of the year when the whole community assembles where there is reliable water and the food it sustains.

so the community can unite, often ostensibly for ritual purposes. Australian Aboriginal life very much fits this pattern. The corroboree is a community assembly for ritual purposes, and these are very important to Aboriginal life. It is very difficult to track the origins and development of this more complex social world in the archaeological record. Even so, as all ethnographically-known forager societies are vertically complex, this complexity very likely predates the last out-of-Africa migration of AMHs. Moreover, if the primitive hominin condition resembled the great ape pattern of suspicion between residential groups, it is also difficult to explain how relatively peaceful relations between communities were established (when, indeed, they were peaceful). Even so, in the next section, I will develop a plausible working hypothesis with some archaeological support.

The argument so far has also taken an individualist approach: cooperation has expanded in the hominin lineage because cooperation has advantaged individual co-operators. There is a line of argument that links the expansion of cooperation to conflict and the threat of conflict between groups. The benefit of cooperation accrues to bands or communities, not the individuals in them, and that is why cooperation has expanded in our lineage. This chapter takes up these themes, beginning by exploring the evidence for cooperation between bands, and then developing an incremental account of the cultural foundations for this increase in the scale of cooperation. In 3.3 and 3.4, I then take up the issues of conflict between bands, the relation between conflict and cooperation, and the question of selection on groups for cooperation. The conclusion about conflict and group selection is cautiously sceptical: we can explain cooperation in terms of individual advantage, though there may well be group-level effects as well. The next chapter turns to the increases in social and economic complexity that began to impact some human communities at the very end of the Pleistocene, and on the implications of those changes for cooperation. More particularly, the focus will be on the origins of sedentary society, the growth of inequality, and the survival of cooperation through that growth. Let's now return to bands, and to the communities composed by culturally affiliated bands; bands that recognize each other as "the same people".

It is important to recognize the striking contrasts between forager bands and great ape residential groups. First, forager bands are residentially open with fluid membership. Individuals and families leave and re-join fairly freely and without resentment. Mothers shift residential groups to visit their daughters and daughters-in-law, especially when they have new babies. Likewise, conflicts are often settled by movement. This open-textured membership co-occurs with, and is supported by, links of mutual support between agents in different bands. Those links are maintained by reciprocity, kinship, and ritual connections.[2] Forager bands are open. They allow movement in and out, and friendly social connections are maintained across bands. *Pan* groups of both species are much more closed. In general adolescent females disperse from chimp and bonobo residential groups, and males stay in the band into which they are born (Stanford 2018). Once females fully leave, they do not return, and for the most part, especially in chimps, civil interactions take place only within the residential group, Bonobo inter-group interactions are much less fraught (Furuichi 2011). But that seems to depend on bonobo females' control of male aggression, which in turn seems to depend on the fact that female bonobos readily form coalitions, while the males do not. If that is true, the ancestral hominin condition was very likely chimp-like. For large and medium game hunting almost certainly involved male coalitions.

Second, bands are part of larger social wholes. A forager band is part of a network of bands, that share a common, mutually and explicitly recognized identity. All or most civil interchange takes place

---

[2] Ritual connection can be surprisingly important. For example, in many Australian aboriginal cultures, connection through the same Dreamtime figure is an important social tie, for it counts as one way of being from the same place (Meggitt 1962).

within that community. That community's identity is typically signalled by a distinctive collective name; by established rights to a territory and its resources. There is often a shared set of ritual practices and beliefs, often including beliefs about the community's common origin; often a distinctive language or dialect, even though many of the individuals in these communities will be multi-lingual (Evans 2017). The community is often the locus of intermarriage, with most pairings drawn from this broader social world. Social trust is often high within the community, but much more contingent beyond it. In some forager cultures the band is the largest unit of collective action (Kelly 2000, Marlowe 2010). But even those bands are part of complex, multi-level communities.

Third, while bands are not composed of close kin, there are extensive kin connections within and across bands (Hill, Walker et al. 2011), and kin connection plays a major organizing role in forager life. Forager life is typically life in a family, co-resident with a small group of other families, but embedded in extensive, explicitly recognized, and normatively important kinship networks. Kinship matters to forager life (and more generally, to life in small pre-state societies). Recognition of kin as kin depends on the culture's explicit norms and systems of kin classification. At one stage in its history, anthropology was dominated by the study of kinship systems. That is no surprise since (a) kinship played such a pivotal role in the organization of life in small, pre-state societies, and (b) kinship systems were often both astoundingly complex[3] and very different from community to community. While those differences are real and important, as Bernard Chapais has emphasized, there are nonetheless common elements to human kinship systems. Three of those common features are important to the establishment of cooperation beyond the limits of the band. (i) Humans recognize far more kin as kin than do the great apes. (ii) Recognizing another human as kin is a prima facie reason for cooperation and/

---

[3] For an extraordinary example, see (Levinson 2006).

or trust. (iii) Recognizing another human as kin does not require that person to be resident in the same band. As Chapais emphasizes, kinship in this distinctive human form opens up a prospective avenue of cooperation across residential bands (Chapais 2008, Chapais 2013, Chapais 2014).

So human residential groups are importantly different from those of great apes. In addition, forager band networks form larger social wholes, and these do not just have a virtual existence. At least in most forager cultures, these communities do occasionally come together physically, and when and if they do, these assemblies are the locus of important but rather intrinsically stable forms of cooperation; forms which do not require much policing. (i) One such form of cooperation is information exchange, for these large assembles share news about the state of the world, social and environmental. Robert Kelly points out that for foragers living in environments that change greatly from year to year, this information is both important and difficult to access, as the areas over which the community might move are very large: one Inuit group keeps track of 250,000 square km; Australia's Pintupi tracked 50,000 square kms; the G/wi of Southern Africa kept note of 20,000 km, and with some knowledge of 200,000 km. These are much larger areas than any forager would use in any year, but part of their risk management strategy is to track these larger areas in case they are needed ((Kelly 2013) p 106). (ii) These larger groups facilitate mate exchange. When bands come together, that is often an occasion for the organization of formal marriages, but no doubt also of less public liaisons that contribute to gene flow across the community. (iii) There are occasions for individuals to renew and strengthen their horizontal connections to individuals in other bands: kin, friends, those with whom they share some ritual connection. (iv) They help resolve conflicts, either by formal mediation with elders and ritual leaders, or less formally by individuals simply moving between bands. (v) There is some trading: by 100 kya, raw materials, or the tools made from them on the spot, were quite regularly being used 100 kilometres or more from their point of origin (Marwick 2003). Perhaps these movements are sometimes a signature of long-distance travel by work parties through friendly land (a form of logistic mobility) or of long seasonal movement by a band as a whole. But these transport distances are probably also a sign of trade networks.

While the origins of community-level cooperation are puzzling, once established, the stability of these forms of community-level cooperation is readily understood. They have a clear benefit, without any systematic temptation to cheat. But foragers sometimes face cooperation and collective actions which, if solved at all, need to be solved by social groups larger than a band, and which do make cheating tempting. Territory defence may be a case in point, but I shall postpone discussion of the connection between cooperation and violence to the next section. My focus here will be on forager civil engineering: on environmental modifications that either make their habitat patch produce more resources of the kind wanted, or which make it easier to harvest those resources. Fire was probably the first tool foragers used to modify their habitat. Its use requires skill and care (Garde, Nadjamerrek et al. 2009), but fire does the work. That contrasts with, for example, drive lines. These are fences which make it possible to harvest game much more efficiently, by funnelling a herd into a position of extreme vulnerability. There are many impressive drive lines from North America, channelling animals even as large as buffalo into a killing zone, or even more brutally and efficiently, over a concealed cliff. These are cliffs invisible to the driven animals until it is too late for the ones at the front to stop in time, with the pressure of those behind pushing them to their death. These drive lines require the construction of hundreds of meters (sometimes more) of robust fencing; very robust, if it is to resist being flattened by large, fearful, angry animals. Building sizable drive lines would be well beyond the resources of a single band. And some are very large: Boyd notes a Whisky Flat sheep trap in Nevada with a fence 2.3 kilometres long, and requiring 5,000, juniper posts for its construction ((Boyd 2018) pp 70–71). There is evidence of Neanderthals driving mammoths over cliffs, but, unsurprisingly given the time depths, no evidence of physical structures; it is possible that fire played the containing and channelling role of fences ((Papagianni and Morse 2015) pp 80–81).

Most of our evidence for these large-scale traps and drive lines is Holocene rather than Pleistocene. That might reflect preservation bias, but it is also possible that the cultural innovations that make cooperation at this scale possible evolved late, and by no means universally amongst forager peoples. George Frison in his work in the west of the United States is particularly impressive on this form of cooperation (Frison 2004). He details the different kinds of drive line and traps for different contexts and different species (for example, closed valley versus sand dune traps for bison), and also shows the great skill needed to site bison cliff traps. He discusses the different construction of pronghorn traps (including a very large one at Fort Bridge, Wyoming, with fences hundreds of meters long (pp 134–135); and even the net traps of mountain sheep. One such net has surprisingly survived, made of juniper bark cordage, 50 + meters long, between 1.5 and 2 meters wide, made from 2 kilometres of cordage, and dated to about 8800 bp (p 165). Frison's detailed archaeology and anthropology illustrates the large social scale of this investment in hunting; the eye for country it required and the profound knowledge of the target species on which success relied. Cumulative cultural learning built both the knowledge on which such hunting depended, and the cultural tools which made coordinating and sharing possible.

Foragers also worked at impressive scales to improve the productivity of their territory. Some examples of Australian Aboriginals' ecological engineering involved very considerable effort and skill. For example, Aboriginal fish traps are sometimes impressively large constructions. The Lake Condah fish trap complex (in Victoria) includes a 3.75 km channel linking two wetlands, thus expanding the area of more or less permanent and eel-friendly water. This complex dates to at least 6.6 kya and is perhaps older. These traps altered local water flows and so silted up. So they required significant investment in their upkeep, not just their construction (McNiven, Crouch et al. 2015). The Lake Condah trap complex is by no means unique: there are coastal stone-walled traps in Tasmania, trapping fish tidally (Stockton 1982), and an impressively large complex on the Barwon River, in northern New South Wales (Woodfield 2000). Given the labour involved in the construction and upkeep of these projects, these show collective action by the community (or perhaps even the ethnolinguistic group), not just a band.

Any increase in the social scale of cooperation is bound to create extra challenges. The coordination problem becomes more difficult. Who is to find, cut, transport and dig in the juniper poles? What will they eat while they are doing all this work, and who is responsible for providing and preparing the food? How long will all this take, and when does the drive line need to be ready for action? These questions have to be answered if the drive line is to be built. Especially in forager societies without formal leadership positions, it is far from obvious how these decisions are to be taken in good time, and without themselves generating conflict (even conflicts so serious as to sabotage the whole plan). So as scale goes up, so do the organizational and logistic challenges. These would be difficult, even if interests, beliefs and cooperative motivations were perfectly aligned. But as we go from band to community (or ethnolinguistic group) we will be further and further from perfect alignment. Individuals will know one another less well, so mutual trust will be less well established. They will not have as much common history, and so be both less prepared for, and less tolerant of, variations in ability and drive ("It is only George. That is the best you can expect"). Even if there is consensus on the overriding need for the drive line, there will be different views about exactly what should be done: its precise size, position and timing. And, of course, since the work is arduous and unrewarding, there will be temptations to slacken off, probably reinforced by suspicions that others are idling. No-one wants to be the sucker. The challenge of collective action at these larger scales seems very considerable, and especially in cultures that work through persuasion rather than command.

Most, perhaps all, mobile foragers are like that. So perhaps it is no surprise that some foragers seem to lack the capacity to organize collective action at any level above bands. Frank Marlowe doubts that the Hadza could, for they have no mechanism for sanctioning free-riding.

In his important book on the origins of war, Ray Kelly distinguishes between two kinds of forager society: simple versus segmented (Kelly 2000). In simple forager societies, kinship is typically traced equally through both parents, the largest unit of social action is the band, and members of a band typically have strong reciprocal relationships with individuals in other bands, mediated by kinship, reciprocal visiting, and gift exchanges. As bands are not themselves composed of close kin, these horizontal relationships are not congruent. Individuals in the same band will have different pathways of social support into and out of different bands. On Kelly's analysis, simple forager societies are typically warless. There is occasional encounter skirmishing if resource droughts push one band into another's patch, but these rarely cause serious casualties. These simple societies contrast with segmented communities, where individual identities are much more aligned into corporate groups. These are clan-like entities, often defined by kinship, but where the role of one parent, usually the father, is much more salient than the other. Clans are often notionally all and only the descendants of a single (not always real) progenitor, often with different family lineages within the clan tracing back to his different sons, actual or fictional. Individuals in clans do have horizontal relationships with those outside it. Australian Aboriginal cultures fit Kelly's picture of segmented society. Even so, Indigenous Australians have independent connections through, for example, shared ritual identity. If two individuals are born in locations associated with, because made by, the same dreamtime figure, they are connected. It is one way of being from the same country (Meggitt 1962). But corporate identity through the clan system is very important (see, for example, (Reid 1983) pp 85–90), and in Australia and elsewhere it is sometimes reinforced by intense and demanding initiation rituals, and further cemented by incremental access to sacred, secret knowledge (Keen 2006, Kelly 2015). As the Australian example shows, some mobile forager societies were segmented. But many are small scale farming societies, or somewhat sedentary foragers whose economy is based on collected and stored resources. These invest very heavily in building corporate identity and corporate loyalty not just through a shared ritual life but through a shared material infrastructure of lodges, men's houses and the like (Flannery and Marcus 2012, Hayden 2014), and sometime maintained by intimidating secret societies (Hayden 2018). Individuals in different bands and villages may be members of the same patrilineal descent group. If so, they know it, care about it and are identified by others in those terms. This segmented, corporate aspect of their social identity is reinforced in many ways, and their standing in these corporate groups is an important part of their social capital.

Kelly thinks that segmented social organization opens the door to war, because the members of one clan group treat the members of another clan group as social equivalents, and that turns an interchange of murder and revenge into war. For while a murderer's relatives might be prepared to overlook the revenge killing of a murderer himself (especially if he is clearly guilty, and by the local mores he over-reacted to whatever prompted his act of killing), they will not overlook the revenge killing of any randomly selected vulnerable member of his patrilineage. And so revenge excites a response that can easily escalate into full-blown raiding and warfare. I suggest a simpler, though complementary, hypothesis. Clan-based corporate identity makes possible the solution of more demanding collective action problems, and at scales larger than that of a single village or band. Clan members have strongly congruent social identities and as a consequence, have aligned material interests, since clan identity mediates their social relations within and across clans. One expression of this potential is the construction of drive lines, fish weirs and improved wetlands: ecological engineering beyond the reach of a single band. Another expression is organized violence. For warfare is a particularly difficult collective action problem. Kelly's plausible hypothesis is that corporate identity is the social tool that makes it possible. This social tool has emerged in some but not all forager societies, and that suggests it has a relatively recent origin. The emergence of clan-like organization is signalled by the archaeological evidence of beyond-the-band collective action noted earlier, and archaeological evidence of collective violence. As we shall see in 3.3, most of that evidence is Holocene, too. In village society, it is signaled archaeologically by a distinctive type of construction, as we shall see in the next chapter. These ideas about cooperation at large social scales are summarised in Table 3.1.

Table 3.1 Cooperation between Bands

Form of Cooperation between Bands	Benefits of Cooperation between Bands
"The peace dividend": passive tolerance between bands coupled with civil individual interaction across bands.	Buffering information loss within bands. Buffering stochastic demographic imbalance within bands. Larger information networks. Resolving conflict within bands by one party shifting out. Expanded female kinship networks in reproductive cooperation: grandmothers, sisters move to kin or vice versa. Larger mate choice networks.
Active but low cost cooperation between bands	Trade and trade-like exchange: direct or indirect access to resources over much larger spatial scales. More formal conflict resolution mechanisms. Risk management in the face of local environmental disturbance through the "social defence" of territories.
Active but high cost cooperation between bands.	Large scale environmental engineering. Collective violence and defence against collective violence (including the credible threat of retaliation).

3.2 The Origins of an Open Society

As noted earlier, it is not too difficult to explain the stability of multi-level forager societies, once they have formed, even setting aside the profits that accrue from solving larger scale collective action problems. For even if successful large scale collective action depends on segmented society, simple forager societies enjoy the reproductive advantages of access to a larger network of potential partners; the benefits of the exchange of information about conditions in the region; the flow of local gossip and opportunities for limiting the costs of conflict. These are all profitable forms of cooperation, without offering much temptation to defect. However, if the ancestral condition of hominin sociality was roughly similar to that of chimps, or even other great apes, divided into closed bands, how did multi-level band society emerge? A best guess here combines a model developed by Robert Layton and colleagues with Bernard Chapais' views about the distinctive role of kin recognition in hominin social evolution. The basic idea is borrowed from Robert Layton, but that idea has a problem for which Chapais provides a plausible solution.

Layton's hypothesis is that the simple forager community—the network of bands of the San or the Hadza—corresponds to *pan* residential groups and thus to the band of early hominin evolution. This ancestral band expanded both in numbers and in space, and through this expansion it slowly fractionated, with the ephemeral foraging partnerships known from chimp and bonobo life gradually becoming more stable, more important, and more cooperative (Layton 2008, Layton and O'Hara 2010, Layton, O'Hara et al. 2012). This expansion was driven by changes in hominin foraging: in particular, by a gradual shift to the ecological niche of an apex predator as hominin diets became more meat-based. Apex predators have low population densities and large range sizes, and mobile foragers that derive a significant fraction of their food from hunting and scavenging are constrained in the same way by their prey populations. Of course, as with all aspects of forager life, there is a good deal of variation. Exceptionally challenging environments like the Australian western desert and the high arctic support as few as one forager to 100 square kilometres; the most productive environments perhaps one forager per square kilometre. A most striking datum is that forager density is significantly less than chimp density in the regions in which they overlap (see table 3.2). So the causal sequence is as follows: cultural learning powers a shift into the predator guild, and that shift in turn drives the evolution of vertical complexity, as the primal band of early foragers expands and fractionates. Forager bands from the ethnographic record are the descendants not of the primal bands of early hominins, but of ephemeral alliances and foraging associations within those primal bands, analogous to ephemeral chimp alliances and foraging parties. These became more important as the community expanded in numbers and range size. As a band expands in numbers and range size, that range size comes to exceed the daily foraging range of individuals in that community. As this process unfolded, it gradually became impossible for the band—at this stage the whole community—to come together at nightly camps. The ephemeral and ad hoc groups of males and

Table 3.2 The Use of Space

	Population density km^2
Chimps	2.5
ake	0.31
	0.28 (Bagandou)
Mbuti	0.17 (N'Dele)
	0.17–0.2
	Home Range size km^2
Chimps (Gombe)	9–12
Chimps (Ngogo)	35
Mbuti	260
Aka	490

females that foraged together (in part for safety, in part for collective effort in hunting and gathering) slowly became the stable, focal arena of cooperation and daily interaction and sharing. Repeated association built the trust and expectations of future interaction that makes cooperation possible. A form of association that exists but plays a relatively minor role in *pan* community life, an ephemeral foraging party, existed in early hominin life too, but very gradually assumed greater importance. It became the nexus of daily cooperation in foraging, sharing, childcare and safety at night. It became the band documented in forager ethnography.

The transition to the apex predator niche would not be possible without cooperation. Mid-Pleistocene hominins lacked the weapons which would allow them to hunt successfully as an individual and the morphology that would allow them to gorge on a kill, protecting them against a run of hunting failures. Chasing meat is a high risk, high reward strategy, and so pooling of catches, together with access to back-up resources, was essential to managing risk. On the Layton-O'Hara picture, foraging and hunting associations that were once ephemeral became the central experience of social association, trust and cooperation. Yet the community-level organization does not disappear. In most places, seasonal variation allows the bands to come together at least briefly, and neighbouring overnight camps encounter each other with some regularity. Selection favoured maintaining those associations: advantages included a larger mate choice market, buffering against demographic accidents of various kinds, informal conflict resolution and perhaps informational exchange. Community size and range size both gradually expanded, as cognitive, motivational and ecological constraints on size withered away, and because there are positive advantages to size. But as the territory and the community expands, travel time constraints force fractionation. Above a certain threshold, the community as a whole can no longer regularly reform. But less frequent interaction remains both possible and beneficial.

Layton's model has one very appealing feature. We no longer have a problem of explaining initial steps away from inter-band hostility in a transition from closed to open social worlds. The ancestral forager community expanded spatially and demographically, and as it did so, it developed an internal structure: ephemeral foraging partnerships became nascent bands became the forager bands of ethnography. Layton's model trades the very difficult problem of explaining how bands with independent and largely hostile histories establish trust, for the much easier problem of explaining how trust is maintained between groups who initially knew each other; whose frequency of interaction has declined; yet who can continue to interact in mutually beneficial ways. However, that remains a serious problem, especially given evidence that when a chimp group fractures, the males in each descendant group do become mutually hostile ((Stanford 2018) chapter 4).

At this point, the distinctive forms of human kin recognition become relevant. Humans recognize far more kin than do the *pan* species. That is in part because we recognize paternal kin; in part because we recognize affines (in-laws) as kin; in part because we keep track of extensive networks of biological connection (grandparents; grandchildren; assorted kinds of uncles, aunts, cousins, nieces and nephews); and in part because of culturally defined kin categories without much echo in genetic connection. It is likely that some of this apparatus depends on language, and so probably played no role early in the emergence of multi-level society. But the recognition of paternal kinship is quite likely early. There are persuasive reasons for thinking that even erectine mothers needed support (Opie and Power 2008). If that support came from fathers, who were then recognized as kin by their children, and vice versa, that would be enough for a much richer network of kin connection. That is important, especially if it was coupled with kinship bonds that did not require co-residence, surviving shifts to other nascent bands. In addition, as argued earlier, Pleistocene hominins were under selection for increasing social tolerance and impulse control. For these were essential elements of an economy based substantially on cooperation and cooperative hunting. So continued affiliation is explained by a general reduction in reactive aggression (Wrangham 2019), combined with the expansion of positive affiliation based on the richer set of kinship ties identified by Chapais.

This analysis suggests that the transition from the closed social worlds characteristic of the great apes species to open bands nested in a larger community began quite early, with the erectines or the more clearly apex hunters, the Heidelbergensians (Stiner 2002). Layton and his colleagues suggest that long distance raw material transport is a proxy for more open networks. If raw material movement regularly and comfortably exceeds the plausible daily movement limits of a band, the social world is probably open enough to allow material resources to flow from one band to another, or for bands to allow movement by others into their territories to harvest stone or ochre (Layton and O'Hara 2010, Layton, O'Hara et al. 2012). This proxy suggests a quite deep origin of open-textured social organization, probably with the Heidelbergensians (about 800 kya). That meshes reasonably well with direct evidence for hunting, especially given that measures of distance are minimum measures. As Stephen Kuhn points out, they are straight-line distances between source and discard, and hence make no allowance for either topography or travel with the tool. So longer distance raw material transport is probably somewhat older than this estimate. Moreover, while there is controversy about the extent of erectine hunting and its centrality to erectine lives, there is little controversy about Heidelbergensian hunting. The idea that this transition began with the Heidelbergensians also meshes reasonably well with another indirect signal of a more open social world. I argued in 1.3 and 1.4 that it is very difficult for innovations to establish regionally, and hence become archaeologically visible, in closed social worlds. There are now some hints in the archaeological record of an upward shift in innovation rates after 800 kya.

If the picture of the emergence of multi-level communities with networked bands painted here is on the right track, we should see increasing evidence for an increase in the tempo of innovation, an expansion of raw material movement distance, and an increased footprint of carnivory in the hominin foraging economy, all taking place at broadly the same time.

The picture here presupposes an incremental account of the transition to multi-level social organization. While some of the benefits of peaceful interaction between bands depend only on reasonable mutual tolerance—for example, allowing passage to quarry stone—others depend on more active and committed forms of cooperation (see table 3.1). One of these is human colonization of very challenging environments. In particular, Clive Gamble has argued that hominin social life changed in important ways with the emergence of durable social networks, with an agent being able to trust that they have a stable place in that durable network (he makes this case most extensively in (Gamble 2013)). These networks allow a release from proximity: an agent, or a group of agents, can travel and forage independently of their community, knowing that when they re-join that community, they will still be recognized as part of it, with their social capital intact. Gamble suggests that the elaboration of recognized and enduring kinship connections was an important foundation of network durability. In his view, the human penetration of very difficult ecosystems depended on these stabilized social networks. Arid lands and the high northern latitudes support very low population densities, typically (especially in arid lands) with very small overnight camps of just a few families. In these low productivity environments, the population has to be highly dispersed in order harvest enough resources for their daily needs. These very challenging environments seem to have been occupied quite late in hominin history; in about the last 50 k years (Gamble 2013). In the medium to long run, these tiny groups would be economically, demographically and informationally unsustainable without stable connections to a larger network. It is hard to see foragers in these environments surviving in the long term without the risk-management, social exchange and information sharing benefits of these larger networks.

So this suggests a couple of temporal bookends. In the earlier forms of multi-level society there was mutual tolerance between bands, some residential flexibility and occasional aggregation into a larger community when seasonal abundance permits it. With this, we might see the benefits of sexual exchange; of informal conflict control, allowing conflicting individuals to move away from one another; and perhaps of some of information sharing. The Heidelbergensians may well have lived in a social world something like this, more networked and open that those of the *pan* species, but not yet with the cultural tools needed for mutual support in hostile environments. Networks of bands that were mutually tolerant, and occasionally came together in (fairly) peaceful aggregations were almost certainly precursors to communities that conceived of themselves as a single people, connected by shared norms, rituals, foundation myths and (often) distinct languages or dialects. Communities with these characteristics were probably necessary for life in arid deserts and the high arctic. For the secure use of these environments probably required explicit and acknowledged mechanisms of reciprocation that allow individuals in one band to call on support, and expect to get it, in the face of serious trouble. Risk management in these demanding environments calls for active cooperation across bands, not just tolerance. Building these forms of active cooperation was probably impossible without something close to full language, explicit norms, culturally amplified kinship systems, ritual and shared ritual identity (Sterelny 2014, Sterelny 2017). It follows that this form of cooperation across bands probably required cognitive and culture tools that were available only to contemporary and near-contemporary hominins. The Hxaro exchange system of Southern Africa is a paradigm: a system of mutual gift exchange which signals and supports the existence of these networks of emergency support (Wiessner 2002a). But so too are so-called universal kinship systems: systems that connect everyone in a particular social universe ((Barnard 2011) pp 80–82).

3.3 Cooperation, Culture and Conflict

On the analysis developed in this essay, the slow assembly of the social and cognitive tools of cooperation made war possible. War is an expression of the capacity for high stakes collective action, which in turn depends on the culturally constructed institutions of some forager societies, and their successors. Seriously lethal conflict between bands depends on the same cultural innovations that makes cooperation between them possible. On an alternative view, war and cooperation coevolved: intergroup conflict and cooperation are causally coupled. This view has been developed by Herb Gintis and Sam Bowles (and their collaborators) in one form (see Bowles and Gintis 2003, Bowles 2008, Bowles and Gintis 2011) and by Rob Boyd, Peter Richerson and their colleagues (especially Joseph Henrich) in another (Richerson, Boyd et al. 2003, Richerson and Boyd 2013, Boyd 2016, Henrich 2016). Their picture builds on Richard Wrangham's view that hominin intergroup interactions were driven by the same dynamics as those responsible for chimp intergroup hostility (Peterson and Wrangham 1997, Wrangham 1999). Relations between chimp groups are almost invariably hostile.[4] Suitable territory is always limited, and hence the resources of neighbouring groups (including the females within them) are always a temptation. So it is always in the interests of a coalition of males in one group to attack and kill an isolated male in another group. If that adjoining group already has fewer males, a further kill

---

[4] The far western Tai community seems to be a partial exception. Males patrol, but lethal violence between groups is much rarer. Patrols sometimes seem targeted on establishing an association with females from a neighbouring group, and there is just a hint of the bonobo practice of sex as a way of managing intercommunity tensions in these encounters between male patrols and neighbouring females: see ((Stanford 2018) p 78).

will increase the favourable ratio of power, perhaps to the point that they can be pushed aside. If the adjoining group has more males, a kill will reduce their advantage, making takeover less likely. So as both sets of theorists see it (with the Boyd-Richerson picture more nuanced), the baseline hominin condition was of a population divided into mutually hostile band-sized groups, under conditions of resource scarcity, perhaps generated by the erratic Pleistocene climate, perhaps by population expansion to carrying capacity.

In such a selective environment, a successful takeover by one group of its neighbour's territory would have dramatic fitness consequences for both sides. It would be a catastrophe for at least the males and infants of the defeated group. It would be a fitness windfall for the winners. As this Hobbesian universe at the level of the bands is supposedly the default state, there would be strong pressure in favour of any variation that increased the probability of success. Most obviously, selection on the level of bands would strongly favour cooperation in attack and defence, and an altruistic willingness to take risks in combat. Bowles and Gintis develop population genetic models to show that in such circumstances, with reasonable assumptions about costs and benefits, a gene for an altruistic willingness to fight could spread. But they think cultural variation between groups is likely to be important too. The Boyd-Richerson picture relies entirely on cultural differences within and between groups. Suppose the cultural practices of a group bond its members more tightly; its practices more effectively inculcate norms of mutual support, and of disgust and shame about cowardice. Its decision-making practices lead to more coordination in attack and defence. Such a group is more likely to prevail, and having prevailed, its daughter groups are likely to have largely the same customs, norms, initiation practices, patterns of decision making. Adjoining groups, having seen the successful community expand, are likely to copy at least some of the expanding group's customs and practices. The segmented societies we noted in 3.1, with their strong norms of corporate identity, and their ways of building those loyalties not just at the band and village level but at larger organization scales, fit this picture of cultures well adapted for conflict. According to this line of reasoning, in a conflict-ridden world there is a form of group selection. Groups whose cultural profile allows them to solve the particularly difficult collective action problem of war prosper at the expense of groups with different cultural profiles. As the groups prosper and spread, so too do their cultural attributes.[5]

I am very sceptical of Wrangham's view of the baseline condition on which this analysis depends, on both analytic and on empirical grounds. The hominin situation is very different from that of chimps, and this reshapes the costs and benefits of permanent hostility. First, it makes the origins of multi-level society even more mysterious. The Bowles-Gintis picture of inter-group relations is one of chimp-like hostility on steroids, as mutual suspicion between residential groups is weaponized. Second, as hominins are bipedal, and as they harvest resources from high in the food chain, hominin territories are huge by comparison to those of chimps, with a much lower population density. Look at the contrast between two forest-dwelling forager groups (the Mbuti and the Aka) and two chimp groups (from (Layton and O'Hara 2010):

Notice that the forager's range sizes are much larger than those of the chimps, even though both chimps and foragers dwell in forests; in roughly similar habitats. As we saw in 3.2, some foragers range over even larger areas, with even lower population densities. Large areas (relative to the population size) cannot be defended by active patrolling of the territory's boundaries (though of course rich patches within it might be). Third, chimps do not track, stalk or ambush. Hominin hunters do, and that makes aggressive patrolling into hostile territory much more dangerous.[6]

---

[5] See (Birch 2017) for one way of making this idea precise.
[6] As Ron Planer has pointed out to me, it is possible that Wrangham's scenario might be a better fit with early hominin evolution, before the emergence of effective weapons, stalking, tracking and ambushing; if so, such situations might have selected for male-male cooperation, perhaps setting up the capacities for power scavenging and ambush hunting.

The worst that can happen to a chimp "patrol" of four or so males is that it will encounter a larger group and will be chased off. They will not be attacked by surprise from ambush. Fourth, as noted in 2.3, weapons technology changes the risk profile, even with say, the standard chimp fatal superiority ratio of 4: 1. A lone spear-armed male caught may well be doomed at such odds, but he has a decent chance of inflicting serious damage. Fifth, the supposed benefits of raiding are not as tempting as the analysis suggests. Mobile foragers do not have much material wealth or food to loot (that changes with sedentary life). Nor would access to women be an automatic advantage. Female chimps raise their offspring without any support from the father. For male chimps, sexual access to an expanded supply of females is *always* a fitness boost. That is not the recent hominin pattern. Fathers typically provide material support, directly or indirectly, and this support matters. So sexual access to a newly widowed set of females (whose infants have also probably been killed) is a fitness boost only if the males can also provide appropriate levels of material support to any children that might be produced. That is not trivial; societies with polygynous marriage with all wives potentially bearing children are not very common in forager societies, though there are certainly exceptions (Hart and Pilling 1960).[7] Finally, Wrangham's analysis ignores the potential peace dividend. This goes beyond the costs of actual conflict and the costs of avoiding dangerous border zones (see table 3.1). For adjoining forager groups can and do help each other manage risk. Ecological disturbances are often patchy and unpredictable (wildfire, for example), and those risks can be partially managed by adjoining groups granting access to a group in trouble, in the

---

[7] I also suspect the costs of having to supervise hostile and vengeful extra wives would not be minor. Supervision is not easy in forager societies, as women cannot be confined to a household or a campsite, given the importance of their own foraging. Moreover, an armed female could probably murder a sleeping or inattentive male. I doubt whether that is physically possible for a female chimp.

expectation that similar permission would be granted to them in need. With this cultural practice, mutual recognition of a group's prior right to its territory is coupled with the expectation that those rights will be exercized generously in times of local stress. Robert Kelly calls this the "social defence" of territory and treats it as the default relation between foragers and their territories (see (Kelly 2013) pp 155–158). This risk management is a form of group-to-group direct reciprocation: one where helping has modest costs but very significant benefits. It is open-ended (no-one knows when or who will need help next), symmetrical, easy to track and police, and so is evolutionarily stable. Here again range size matters: chimp territories are smaller and more densely packed, and so it is more likely that hard times in one band's territory are hard times with the neighbours too.

The empirical data match these analytic considerations. There is no skeletal evidence from Pleistocene foragers suggesting that those foragers were resource stressed, living close to the bone (no evidence of widespread dietary deficiency, for example). As we saw at the end of 3.2, humans do not seem to have lived in the most marginal habitats until about 50 kya. Likewise, Flannery's Broad Spectrum Revolution, with its evidence of human exploitation of low return resources, is very late Pleistocene (about 20 kya, in the Middle East) (Flannery 1969, Zeder 2012). While this evidence is far from decisive, it suggests that for almost the whole of the Pleistocene, resource stress did not force hominins into dependence on low value habitats or low value resources. That is no surprise, for the concept of a natural carrying capacity setting a hard limit on population size does not apply well to populations that actively manage their habitats, as foragers do.

There is direct evidence of violence, but it is late. There are human remains that look very much like the outcome of massacre or battle: a number of bodies found together, with skeletal evidence of multiple wounds. But the earliest of these sites are at the very end of the Pleistocene, when the shift to a more sedentary lifeway was beginning (Flannery and Marcus 2012, Kim and Kissel 2017). There is no evidence through the Pleistocene that camp sites were chosen with defence in mind. Those that we have found seem to have been selected for shelter and convenient access to water and other resources (Finlayson 2014). There is no Pleistocene evidence of weapons made for war. Perhaps we should not expect such evidence, even if war was common. For in the archaeological record, hunting and military technology would look much the same (Pleistocene leather and wood shields would not survive). But Neolithic archaeologists treat sling-stones as anti-personal weapons, not hunting weapons, and sling-stones have not been found in Pleistocene sites. There is cave art from about 35 kya, and through almost all the Pleistocene, there are no depictions of war. Depictions of animals, hunting and sex abound, but not violence (Guthrie 2005). Of course the evidence we have is very patchy and might be misleading. As (Kim and Kissel 2017) rightly note, a good deal of Pleistocene conflict would be archaeologically invisible. But the evidence we have does not suggest a militarized Pleistocene.

I am not suggesting that the human world of the Pleistocene was a world of endless peace. I would be utterly astounded to learn that interactions between Pleistocene forager groups were always peaceful. Conflicts over resources; conflicts over sex; just plain hot-blooded ill-temper must sometimes have got out of hand, for the same reason that murder rates in mobile forager societies are high. There are no institutional mechanisms that can authoritatively intervene when tensions are rising, to impose peace (Boehm 2000, Boehm 2012). I do not think the Pleistocene was free of inter-group conflict, and I suspect that on occasions, some conflicts caused serious casualties. Rather, my views are (i) tension and violence was not the standing state of group–group interactions through the Pleistocene. Relations were often civil, or better. (ii) Hence intercommunal violence and its threat did not result in strong pressure at the level of groups for cooperative norms and customs, especially norms and customs that made groups more effective in attack and defence. If through much of the Pleistocene, mobile foragers had been under selection for military efficiency, we would expect to see norms and attitudes that favour command-and-control decision making within the collective. That is not what we see. We have ethnographic evidence of the norms that emerge in the context of high rates of intercommunity violence, and they are very different from those typical of mobile foragers. When the threat of intercommunity violence is strong we observe a very different social organisation, with family ties downplayed and male–male associations foregrounded (see (Rodseth 2012)). In contrast, the norms typical of mobile forager cultures emphasize the autonomy of individual decision making, rejecting the idea that any individual has the authority to issue commands. (iii) Strong selection on groups is not needed to explain cooperative norms and practices within groups. In general, acting cooperatively maximizes individual fitness, through the fitness rewards of a good reputation. (iv) While there is no clear evidence that demonstrates it, I am open to the possibility that cultural group selection played a significant role in explaining the new and more complex social lives that date from late in the Pleistocene. It is, for example, possible that segmented communities are common because they out-competed unsegmented communities through their superior abilities to organize larger scale collective action, including war. One puzzle about Australian ethnography is the dominance of the Pama-Nyungan language family over much of the continent, and one hypothesis is that the language family is associated with a particular form of social segmentation: see (Henrich 2016) pp 176–180, for one version of this idea. In the next section, I lay out some of the framework for this set of ideas, before turning in chapter 4 to the social transformations of the very late Pleistocene.

3.4 Individual Selection, Group Selection and Cultural Group Selection

In the book to this point, I have suggested that cooperation has, on average, been advantageous for individual co-operators. Cooperation has evolved by selection on individuals in virtue of benefit to that individual. Cooperation is profitable but not altruistic. As we have seen earlier in discussing the connection between cooperation and violence, that is not the only view in town. Cooperation, because it is costly, has often been seen as individually altruistic, and so it has been supposed that we can explain its origin and stability only because altruistic individuals benefit the groups within which they reside, and that group beneficial effect explains the origin and persistence of costly, hence altruistic, cooperation. Famously, even Darwin, in *The Descent of Man* (p 130) was attracted to this idea.

> When two tribes of primeval man, living in the same country, came into competition, if . . . the one tribe included a great number of courageous, sympathetic and faithful members, who were always ready to warn each other of danger, to aid and defend each other, this tribe would succeed better and conquer the other.

However, in analyses of the evolution of cooperation, group selection has played a complex, tangled and controversial role. It has been proposed (i) as an explanation of patterns of behaviour that are individually altruistic, imposing on the agent a net lifetime cost, but which are beneficial to the social group, and (ii) as an explanation of phenomena that are characteristics of groups, rather than of individuals within the group. Having a clan-based social organization is a feature of a community, not of individuals within the community. More recently, it has been proposed (iii) as an explanation of the distribution of norms and customs across a population of groups. In particular, it is supposed to explain why many norms of many societies are prosocial. That distribution calls for explanation (according to this line of thinking, which we discussed in 2.4) because norm-driven punishment can stabilize a huge variety of norms, including destructive ones (Boyd and Richerson 1992, Henrich 2016). If the costs of punishment are high, it is individually adaptive to conform to patterns of action that would otherwise be seriously maladaptive. Foot-binding in traditional Chinese society is a presumptive example. As this example shows, socially destructive norms exist. But, the argument goes, they are relatively rare because selection between groups penalizes the communities in which they establish.

So there are differing ideas on what group selection might explain (for masterly analyses of these various forms of group selection, see (Okasha 2006, Godfrey-Smith 2009, Birch 2017). These hypotheses also differ in their selective mechanism, in the way fitness is conceptualized. One group might be fitter than another because the individuals in the group, in virtue of being in that group, are on average fitter than individuals in neighbouring groups. Life in that group confers an advantage to the individuals in it, and fitness is individual productivity. When those offspring disperse to form new groups, they will tend to have the same traits as those that made their natal group more productive. This is known as "multi-level selection 1" (MLS 1). Alternatively, a group might be fitter than its neighbours because it is less likely to go extinct and/or more likely to found new groups (like itself). Here as we count winners and losers, we are counting groups, not persons. This is multi-level selection 2 (MLS 2).

Group selective explanations of cooperation are intuitively plausible, because some cooperative actions seem to be very individually costly and yet strikingly beneficial for the group the agent helps: the heroic lone stand that lets everyone else escape. For the last fifty years, sparked by one of the great classics of evolutionary thinking (Williams 1966), evolutionary biologists have been mostly sceptical of group selection. One reason for this scepticism is that it is surprisingly difficult to show that there is altruism in humans, in the sense relevant to evolutionary theory. For we do not give evolutionary explanations of *particular acts*, but of patterns of action, dispositions to act in certain ways in certain context. These are behavioural strategies (Birch 2017). A behavioural strategy can on average benefit the agent who adopts it, even if on some occasions it is spectacularly expensive. Heroism in battle that ends in death but delivers victory might seem obviously altruistic: a lifetime cost to the agent, but a major benefit to his community. But if live heroes are spectacularly rewarded, heroism might be a high risk, higher reward strategy that for the right agent, on average, pays off. So while there are clearly *acts* that benefit a community and that cost the agent far more than he/she gains, it is not obvious that there are altruistic *strategies*. But the main reason for scepticism has been the problem of subversion from within. Let's accept that groups composed of altruists will do better than those composed of the selfish. But what happens in mixed groups? That matters, because natural processes generate variation in groups through migration and mutation, and so we expect groups to become mixed. In a mixed group, S-individuals[8] do better than A-individuals, because they have advantages of living in a cooperative group without paying the costs; they defect. There is a race between group selection favouring altruism at the level of groups, and individual selection undermining altruism in mixed groups. In principle, group selection can win the race. But that requires S-types to arise in altruist groups very rarely, and for it to be difficult for S-types to migrate into altruistic groups. The standard line of argument was that individual selection will almost always swamp group selection (though this has become more contested over time).

Adding cultural learning and cultural inheritance to this analysis changes the dynamics in important ways. Hence the focus in much recent literature on cultural group selection as an explanation of

---

[8] S=Selfish; A=Altruistic.

cooperation. Once cultural learning becomes a pervasive feature of human environments: (i) it tends to make groups, and social networks more generally, more internally homogenous, especially if individuals tend to absorb the practices and customs typical of their group.[9] (ii) It tends to make groups differ from one another, as accidental early differences in customs and norms become entrenched as specific local traditions. Moreover, compared to genetic evolution, these differences appear quickly (Richerson and Boyd 2001, Boyd 2016). (iii) It tends to increase the difficulty of migration, especially between ethnolinguistic groups. As the variation between groups goes up, it is harder to adapt to life in the new group because its mores, customs and language are all different and all must be learned. Even if the migrant is accepted, there is a lot to learn, and acceptance is often conditional on the migrant accepting the customs of his/her new community. Pervasive cultural learning tends to generate greater differences between groups and fewer differences within groups. For in contrast to purely genetic models, migration between groups may not generate variation within groups. It does not, if migrants are induced to conform to the practices of the groups they join. These are conditions which make group selection more powerful. For it has more variation to work with, and individual selection is less powerful, as there are fewer differences within groups. Even genetic differences are somewhat masked by conformist cultural learning; genotype difference translates less into phenotype difference. This is cultural group selection because cultural learning explains both the increased variation across groups and the reduced variation within them.

So understood, it is quite possible that cultural group selection has played an important role in human evolution. I have argued, however, that we do not need it to explain the origins or stability of mutualist cooperation or reciprocation in the Pleistocene. In the

---

[9] Either by some form of conformist learning, or where everyone tends to learn from a couple of the most prestigious individuals in the group.

next chapter, we come to the stability of cooperation through the more complex and less equal social worlds that appear around the Pleistocene/Holocene boundary, about 12 kya. In my view, there is no clear evidence that group selection drove social change in the early Holocene. But it may have been influential. At this point, conflict between groups is clearly becoming important, and that makes group selection a plausible mechanism of change. We may need it to explain the spread of segmented communities, if they spread at the expense of simple bands in virtue of their capacity to organize collective action at larger scales. This would be an instance of our second explanatory target: a group selective explanation of a trait of a group. Evolutionary theorists have been sceptical of this too: they see group-level properties as aggregate outcomes of selection acting on individuals within groups. In G.C. Williams' vivid example, a herd of horses is fast because the individual horses have been selected for speed. Analogously, an individual selection account of segmentation would look for factors which would favour individuals beginning to prioritize the set of relatives they are connected with through the male line, and to invest more heavily in maintaining and strengthening those connections. In very rough outline, one can see how such a change might take place through an arms race: once one group of patrilineally-linked individuals began to organize itself as a proto-clan, with the collective clout of a nascent clan, others were compelled to respond in kind. A particular kind of social capital would become critical to individual fitness. Individuals with that form of social capital, with their capacity to solve challenging collective action problems have individual fitness gains at the expense of others. Those others would then themselves be incentivized to prioritize their own paternal kin connections. We return to these issues of group selection and the role of conflict between groups in 4.2.

In this chapter, the focus changed from interaction within bands to interaction between bands. One form of interaction is conflict, and the chapter discusses an influential view of the

Pleistocene: conflict was common, a standing threat, and that threat shaped social life within bands through some form of group selection. The chapter is sceptical of that view of the Pleistocene, but it may well have some validity for the Holocene. The positive theme of the chapter is its account of the emergence of cooperative relations between bands, probably beginning with the Heidelbergensians, but becoming richer and more stable over the next 800 k years. These socially and spatially extended forms of cooperation depended on cognitive and cultural tools built by iterated cultural learning. Of these, the culturally-mediated expansion of kin recognition, and its transformation in some communities into clan-like corporate organization, is probably the most important.

4
Cooperation in Hierarchical Communities

4.1 The Puzzle of Farming

Beginning towards the end of the Pleistocene, around 12 kya, in many parts of the world, human life began to change dramatically. Life on the move began to be replaced by settled life; wild resources began to be supplemented, then largely replaced, by domesticated resources. The scale of social life increased, and social worlds became less equal. Through this profound revolution, cooperation continued and perhaps even expanded. Moreover, cooperation in these early hierarchical societies did not depend on organized coercion of the kind available to early states and chiefdoms. These were "transegalitarian" communities, to borrow Hayden's term. There were significant differences in power and wealth, but leadership was not yet hereditary, and formal institutions of coercion and command had not yet established. Furthermore, elites lived in close proximity to the rest, and hence were vulnerable to physical measures of the kinds that suppressed hierarchy in mobile forager cultures. That said, direct coercion may well have been important on occasion. Hayden documents extensive ethnographic evidence of secret societies in these transegalitarian communities and their recourse to coercion and intimidation (Hayden 2018).

To understand these changes, we must identify the interactions between:

1. the establishment of a more sedentary society
2. an economy based on farming (and/or herding)

3. a steep increase in demographic scale with more specialization and trade
4. the establishment of social worlds which were not just larger and more complex, but which were seriously unequal.

The transition from life as a mobile forager to life in settled society based on domestication was once conceptualized as a unified package deal, linking the domestication of plants and animals to a sedentary life style, storage, craft specialization and trade, and the use of pottery; a package that also marked the first stages of a transition to civilized life. This was the Neolithic Revolution (Childe 1936). It turns out that some of these changes had their origins deep in the Pleistocene, whereas others, like pottery, became important only in the late Neolithic. The "Neolithic package" was less tightly integrated, and with its origins spread over more time than Childe supposed. Even so, he was right to identify a profound social transition here, one much more puzzling than he realized. Through these complex interactions, the social contract survived, even though the demands of collective action were often more intense in early Neolithic worlds than those that faced foragers. Land had to be cleared; the land had to be fenced (or protected in some other way); often irrigated and fertilized; crops had to be weeded and protected from pests and competitors. Storage facilities had to be built. In many places, as intercommunal tensions rose, villages had to invest in protection: in village walls and ditches, in weapons. Many early farming societies invested heavily in public buildings and in expensive displays, perhaps to deter prospective enemies and impress prospective allies (Seabright 2010, Flannery and Marcus 2012). While I doubt that Pleistocene social worlds were structured by inter-group violence, this threat was *very serious* for many early villages.

The origins of farming and the Neolithic transition were once seen as a human triumph. It was abandoning a life of impoverished wandering, at the mercy of nature, to begin on the path to civilization, with control over your own food supply; the beginnings of trade and craft specialization; even before metal, it saw finer and more varied tools, with edge-ground rather than flaked blades; with pottery and storage; sleeping with a roof over your head and walls to keep the wind and rain at bay, rather than being at the mercy of the elements. Of course foragers took up farming as soon as they could, as soon as they knew how. On this view the problem explaining the origin of farming is the problem of explaining why it took so long. Marshall Sahlins' *The Original Affluent Society* was both signal and cause of a revolutionary change in view. Sahlins and others argued that foragers had good lives (Sahlins 1968, Diamond 1987). They gathered what they needed in a few hours, so had plenty of leisure; they had effective risk management through mobility and a broad resource portfolio. Once the danger of childhood disease was over, they had a reasonable life expectancy; they had good dental health and were free of dietary deficiency diseases. In contrast, the life of early farmers was one of long, arduous, unrewarding work. They were very seriously exposed to risk, with a narrow resource portfolio; with crops vulnerable to pests, raids and adverse weather and with movement having very high costs. Their narrow diet had adverse health consequences (their dental health was often horrible), and so too did their sedentary life. Foragers leave their excrement behind; farmers live amongst it (Scott 2017). Very likely, Sahlins exaggerated the ease of forager life (Kelly 2013), but even so, the adoption of farming looks puzzling once we recognize its grinding nature.

Let me give the bare bones of what I take to be the best model of the origin and establishment of farming,[1] though the crucial issue in the argument that follows concerns the effects rather than the

---

[1] For a fine overview of the debates about the origins of farming and their history, see chapter 1 of (Barker 2006). For the most sophisticated version of the view that farming's origins lay in political rather than subsistence needs, see (Hayden 2014). For a recent review of its demographic dynamics and its spread into Europe, see Shennan, S. (2018). *The First Farmers of Europe: An Evolutionary Perspective*. Cambridge, Cambridge University Press.

origins of the first farming: the changes farming and its prequels wrought in the social lives of farmers. The central hypothesis is that farming developed incrementally from storage-based foraging as individuals adjust adaptively to their slowly changing local circumstances (Testart, Forbis et al. 1982, Watkins 2010, Sterelny 2015, Sterelny and Watkins 2015). Storage foraging typically develops when the following conditions appear:

1. Predictable and large seasonal variation in resource availability.
2. Abundant resources in the high season.
3. A seasonal spike that can be harvested efficiently.
4. A seasonal surplus that can be stored with low wastage and little risk.

In sum: for storage to become important, the seasonal boom must be coupled with efficient harvest and safe storage. Once foragers have begun to harvest and store seasonal resource booms, that sets the stage for farming. For storage foragers (i) are somewhat sedentary; (ii) they have already developed the technology and techniques to process and store food not needed for immediate consumption; (iii) they are adapted to year-long planning cycles; (iv) they are exposed to some of the same social risks as farmers. Stored food, whether collected or farmed, is a conflict flash point. It is a flash point between communities, because stored food is a tempting target for inter-communal raiding, and locally because the shift to a more sedentary life makes it possible for individuals and families to accumulate more material goods. These too will be valuable to others. (v) They have begun the transition from managing risk by mobility and a broad resource portfolio to betting on the reliability of their storage technology. (vi) Storage foragers have a season when they draw on their resources, and hence have time available to manage and alter their local surrounds; there will be little opportunity cost in investing in the land and its improvement.

(vii) Storage foraging sometimes leads to significant social inequality, often comparable with that seen in early farming worlds. The Pacific Northwest is an ethnographically documented example ((Kelly 2013) chapter 9), and there is archaeological evidence on such inequality in glacial Europe, presumably based on stores of frozen, hunted meat (Kuzmin, Burr et al. 2004).[2]

Once foragers have become more sedentary and more dependent on their stores, where the ecology allows it, there is a smooth, incremental, almost imperceptible pathway to farming. Each step reduces risk or increases supply by low-cost interventions. Each additional increment in fields, places or stock is a small change, yielding a modest additional yield from managed resources. But cumulatively, though perhaps over many generations, dependence on produced or managed food increases, and so does the cost of movement. As with the transition to a semi-sedentary mixed economy from mobile foraging, this may often have been a slow process. Even so, as communities proceed on this pathway from foraging to farming, stresses on the Pleistocene social contract accumulate.

1. Storage foraging has demographic effects. Since it smooths the effect of seasonal variation, it reduces the impact of the season of scarcity on community size. Moreover, sedentary life increases fertility, because mothers (or helpers) no longer have to carry infants to new campsites as the group moves. These production systems often deliver food more easily digested by weanlings, also easing constraints on inter-birth intervals. So there is likely to be local population growth, an

---

[2] Though there is an alternative explanation in terms of seasonality, for there are examples of foragers that disperse into small groups in some seasons, and aggregate into larger and much more socially complex groups in others. So the glacial record might be traces of a seasonally plastic social world: the rich symbolic life was an aspect of the complex, larger, aggregation phase, when bands came together at migratory choke points, to harvest (but not store) the seasonal flood, dispersing into smaller, less archaeologically obtrusive groups in other seasons (Wengrow and Graeber 2015). Australia's foragers used episodic booms in (for example) bunya pine kernels to support these larger social aggregations, rather than storing them for long term use (Gould 1980).

effect which intensifies with farming. The gradual shift to farming both draws resources from lower in the food web, and suppresses competition from weeds. So a larger fraction of total productivity is secured for human use.

2. Storage and farming are more akin to gathering than hunting: Forager norms of sharing apply less universally to gathered foods, as gathering is less at the mercy of bad luck. The flow of gathered resources is likely to reflect differences in skill and commitment, and so the highly skilled and hardworking will have less reason to share. They do not need to insure themselves against risks of failure they cannot control. Norms of sharing are also in danger of erosion because storage increases the value of possession, and so increases the cost of sharing. "Tolerated theft" explanations of demand sharing rely on the idea that once an agent in possession has satisfied his/her immediate needs, the value of the remaining food to its owner declines sharply. But if food can be stored, that is not true. In any case, farmed resources are not of the kind so routinely shared in many forager communities, and for that reason, norms of equality and sharing may well erode.

3. Farming also encourages a shift to norms that respect property rights and to formal or informal sanctions for violating them (Bowles and Choi 2013, Gintis 2013). Farmers invest in their farms and crops: initially, by holding back seed to plant, and then clearing land, in preparing and improving soils; in tending crops; in investing in tools to plant, harvest, process, and store produce. They invest in a built environment, not just in their lands and crops. These investments in crops and buildings would be profoundly irrational without secure possession of the product. Property rights function as guarantees of secure possession. Farming thus encourages the privatization of economic life, as investment, production, and storage become more family centred and less community based. It is true that land could be farmed in common, and there is some

archaeological evidence of communal storage in some early farming communities. But differences in skill, commitment, and demand for the product would make such a commons conflict prone.
4. Once something like private property in farmed land (or managed flocks) is recognized, a similar dynamic will tend to make the right of possession heritable. Limited ownership land tenure systems are possible—systems in which a farmer has exclusive right to a block of land, and its products, but with that right becoming void at his/her death. Within such a system, land is not heritable, and so wealth differences in a farming culture will not accumulate across generations. Some traditional leasehold systems work a bit like this. But once property rights in land are recognized, those rights will tend to recognize inheritance. For humans have overlapping rather than discrete generations. Subsistence farmers work the land with their offspring, and so their combined investment across a generation is part of the value of the land, part of its productivity. If property rights exist to make investment in land secure enough to make such investment rational, they will tend to recognize transfer rights to the next generation. For otherwise farmers' children will be incentivized to disperse to clear fallow land, rather than work, preserve and improve existing holdings.
5. As this dynamic continues within communities, relations between communities are likely to become more stressed, with conflict a greater threat. Sedentary communities are resource hotspots, so the rewards of aggression are greater, while the costs of defence are likewise worth paying. Moreover, to the extent that these transitions are driven by real or socially-generated resource stresses,[3] the "social defense" of territory

---

[3] I have in mind Hayden's idea that competitive displays within and between communities generates an escalating demand for resources, independently of simple subsistence needs.

will be less stable. The costs of helping another community in need are higher, and the temptation to renege on previous help is stronger. All these potential stresses would be exacerbated by population growth, with communities being more densely packed, with the resulting ambiguities about border zones, and perhaps competition for the more fertile patches of land.

So here is the picture in a nutshell. Foraging depletes the resources available to foragers—sometimes imperceptibly, sometimes not. The more skilled and efficient they are, all else equal, the more rapidly they deplete their most favoured resources. The result was the "broad spectrum revolution" (Flannery 1969). Foragers expanded their resource envelope, often developing new tools and techniques. In favourable environments, that expansion included harvesting and storing seasonally abundant resources. That, in turn, led to a more sedentary life, an expanded population, and selection for still more intense use of available resources. In some places, where there were suitable plants, intensification could develop by enriching the local environment: seeding it with suitable plants, and perhaps managing those local patches to increase their value (e.g., using fire to clear weeds before planting). These probably began as low-cost measures.[4] The initial labour costs were not intrinsically high, and they may have been paid by children and others not central to the flow of foraged resources. However, an expanded, sedentary population intensively exploiting wild resources in the local region will eventually have a deep ecological footprint. Over time, but often many generations, relative importance shifted from opportunistically exploiting wild resources in chance encounters, to intensively targeted and stored wild resources, and thence to managed

---

[4] Very low cost, if it began by exploiting seasonably predictable river floods, planting seed in the fresh silts left as floods receded; see James Scott's *Against the Grain*, for this suggestion in the context of reaffirming the Sahlins-Diamond line about life as a forager.

resources (Zeder 2011). Once foragers abandon movement and invest in place, if potential domesticates are available, it is very likely that there will be an incremental slide to farming.

At each stage, agents are making minor and sensible adjustments to their lifeways. But the cumulative effect of those sensible decisions leaves agents at the end of the chain with fewer options, a more rigid social environment and exposed to a very different set of risks. This occurs in a world where cooperation is still important, but where many of the mechanisms which once sustained that cooperation are weaker or absent. Moreover, Robert Kelly points out that once a sedentary way of life is established in a few places, it is apt to spread rapidly. For sedentary communities establish initially in the most productive spots, and as these become off-limits to those still living as mobile foragers, the option of remaining mobile becomes less rewarding, pushing others towards a similar transition ((Kelly 2013) chapter 9). Finally, as Brian Hayden has emphasized, storage foraging and/or farming has the potential to generate a surplus, and that potential will quite often be realized. For storage foragers and farmers have an incentive to produce and store more than they expect to need, as a risk management strategy. Once that surplus exists, it is available for social purposes, to build the social capital of those who control it (Hayden 2014).

By no means all storage forager groups transitioned to agriculture. In particular, in the Americas, storage was often storage of marine resources. Most famously in the Pacific Northwest, sedentary and semi-sedentary communities developed around salmon harvesting, taking advantage of the seasonal runs as salmon returned to their natal stream to spawn. As noted, some of those communities developed significant size and social hierarchy (including slave holding), with family or clan-based ownership of rich salmon harvesting sites. In virtue of such ownership, some families (or clans) were much more wealthy and influential than others. It is hard to explain the collective recognition of private ownership of these sites. It is true that there was investment in these rich sites through the construction of fish weirs, improving the harvest. But in contrast to arable but as yet uncleared land, these rich runs are valuable resources *independently* of extra investment. They do not require that investment to turn them into valuable social resources. With farmed land, one might see ownership in return for clearing and improvement as a rational bargain between the many and the owners. But recognizing ownership of a rich salmon run in return for improving the harvest rate would be a terrible deal for the many. One view, borrowing from the evolutionary ecology of animal behaviour, is that we should expect individual possession (by the fittest and the strongest) of resources that are predictably located, rich, and dense. Such resource islands are both defensible and worth defending. This might explain collective defence by a community of its territory. But, strictly speaking, none of these salmon runs are defensible by an individual, family or even clan, if they have to be defended against the rest of the community. Secure possession depends on the consent of the rest, even if that consent is reluctant, grudging, contingent.[5] Possession is a cultural fact, not a reflection of raw coercive power (which is not to saw that raw coercive power was irrelevant). Why is consent granted from the majority to the minority? We turn to this in the next two sections.

4.2 Cooperation in an Unequal World

Recall from 2.1 that perhaps the most robust result of both theoretical modelling and the experimental work of behavioural economics is that cooperation crashes if there is uncontrolled defection. Likewise, the message of the literature on social preference

---

[5] This is a serious challenge to the model of the evolution of inequality defended in (Mattison, Smith et al. 2016). In modelling the options of the less wealthy, they consider only cutting a deal with the elite, accepting subordination, or individual migration. But the most serious problem is to explain why subordinates do not take collective action against elites. They simply do not model that option.

is that agents typically enter social interactions with a default in favour of cooperation, but with a strong dislike of being taken for a sucker. They resent cheats and are willing to punish them at some cost. These results sit very oddly with much of the last ten thousand years of human history. From the perspective of both theory and experiment, the survival of the social contract through the Holocene is deeply paradoxical. For in much of the Holocene, most humans have lived in profoundly unequal societies, societies in which a very large fraction of the social surplus is creamed off by elites, leaving much of population with not much more than a bare subsistence. All the agrarian states of China, India, Central and South America, Mesopotamia, and the Mediterranean were kleptocracies. These are societies in which defection has run wild. And yet the poor continued to contribute to collective action positively and negatively: positively, paying taxes, helping to build public infrastructure, serving in armies; negatively, by not going feral.[6] In the light of theory and experiment, why did the social contract survive, for the most part, in most places, in an unequal world?

Perhaps once the first efficient states emerged, there is an easy answer to this question: overwhelming coercive power made submission to wretched subordination the least worst option. Even if that is right,[7] states with an efficient coercive apparatus are the products of hundreds or thousands of years of an increase in size, vertical complexity and organizational control. No collective goes from an egalitarian community to a policed state in one step. States are the result of cumulative social changes. Inequality becomes entrenched in communities, and some of these were stable enough and cooperative enough to eventually grow into centralized states (by some

---

[6] Occasionally complex societies atomized, collapsing into banditry, but not routinely, in every highly unequal society.

[7] Paul Seabright argues, I think convincingly, that even in the most efficiently policed community, coercion cannot do all the explanatory work (in part because of the problem of coercing the coercers) Seabright, P. (2006). "The evolution of fairness norms: an essay on Ken Binmore's Natural Justice." *Politics Philosophy And Economics* 5(1): 33–50.

mixture of growth, fusion and take-over). In the pre-state period, when these communities were unequal and hierarchical, the survival of cooperation and the social contract cannot have rested on the efficient coercion of the majority by a minority. We are thus faced with two questions: (1) How and why did egalitarian forager communities sometimes become unequal, hierarchical societies? (2) Why did cooperation and collective action survive that change?

In answering these questions, it is important to remember that the egalitarian world of mobile foragers required active policing. Chris Boehm's work on forager politics and forager norms repeatedly emphasizes this point (Boehm 1999, Boehm 2012), as does (Artemova 2016). Forager communities regularly included aggrandizers: those with a disposition to tell others what to do; with a disposition to hog the limelight; with a disposition to corner as much as they could of whatever was available. In forager communities the tensions induced by these individuals were usually contained by low key verbal policing: jokes, teasing, mocking. Occasionally stronger methods were deployed (one of which was just moving away). Very occasionally a really intractable individual was killed, though this sanction seems to have mostly been targeted at the habitually violent. The point is that egalitarianism did not just persist, it was enforced. In my view, the capacity to enforce egalitarianism eroded in these more sedentary communities through the collective impact of three factors acting in parallel. One set of factors concerned changes in the economic organization of sedentary societies and their immediate consequences. Another concerned changes in the political environment as communities switched from a mobile to a settled lifeway. The third were changes in the social environment that made bottom-up collective action problems more challenging. These structural changes were supported by and reflected in ideological changes and the institutions that supported community ideology, changes discussed in 4.3.

The Economics of Hierarchy. In the last section, I noted that once there is private property in subsistence resources with inheritance, unless there is some countervailing mechanism, inequalities in wealth will tend to grow over time. Imagine, contrary to fact that there was a Generation One, in which private property is for the first time recognized, uniformly across the community, and with everyone beginning with an equal value chunk of land (or wetland, or salmon run, or herd of domestic animals). Natural variations in strength, health, lifespan, and focus will cause variations in the improved value of individual property, as will the luck of external disturbance on both the land itself, and crops and stores drawn from it. Herders are particularly at risk from external troubles. Natural and human disasters can wipe out their whole stock. Moreover, variations in Generation One fertility will make a difference to the initial endowment of the next generation (see (Morris 2015) for a clear exposition of this point). A farmer with six children must either discriminate, impoverishing some, or fractionate his holdings. A farmer with one son has no such dilemma. Of course, children can be a resource too. If labour is scarcer than land, the six children in the next generation will allow the farmer to expand his holdings, and it is the low fertility farmer who is at risk. Context affects the impact of variation, but natural variation will ensure that in Generation Two some will start ahead in the race, and others behind. Those ahead will sometimes be able to use their initial advantage to leverage a further improvement: perhaps through the obligations of debt on someone unable to feed their family from a small plot in a bad year. Unless there is some redistribution mechanism, the initial impacts of luck will tend to be amplified rather than dampened. Demand sharing cultures share as of right, so those whose resources are topped up incur no debt obligation. But we are less likely to see demand sharing in a community organized around storage foraging, for with storage comes a tendency to manage risk through family stores rather than resource pooling. The factors making the recognition of inherited property rights more likely also weaken redistributive norms.

The take home message: once there is recognition of private property in subsistence resources coupled with the right of inheritance, wealth inequalities tend to grow. As we shall now see, in a world with serious risks of intercommunity conflict, wealth can be transformed into power and influence, and then into more wealth.

The Political Opportunities of Conflict. The shift from a mobile to a sedentary lifeway made the political environment more competitive and conflicted. One aspect of this change was an increasing footprint of intercommunity violence. War was an important aspect of pre-state politics in the Holocene; not everywhere; not always, but in enough places and times to make peace precarious and relations between communities tense. This threat, the existence of fraught relations between communities, offered incipient elites within communities an opportunity, and not just because military operations themselves favour top-down decision-making customs. For these incipient elites can use their extra material and social resources to make themselves the mediators of intercommunity interaction and negotiation ((Kelly 2013) chapter 9). Both ethnography and archaeology show that as social worlds became sedentary, larger and more complex, there was heavy investment in costly signals (reviewed in (Flannery and Marcus 2012, Hayden 2014)). Some of this took the form of investment in public buildings, usually buildings with important ritual functions. But feasts were another important signal in these sedentary communities, often with lavish gift-giving. The potlatch feasts of the Pacific Northwest are paradigm examples, but the same phenomenon is found in Polynesian and Melanesian societies (see (Knauft 2005) for a vivid Melanesian example). To the extent that these feasts and displays are signals, they are in part signals from the sponsors and organizers of these performances, not just from the communities as a whole, and they are signals to peers in communities that are potentially both rivals and allies, not just to those communities as a whole. By organising, sponsoring, and in part paying for expensive displays, wealthier members of a community can advertise their influence, their capacity to move and shake, to others like them in neighbouring communities. Given the genuine threat and high risks of inter-community violence, and the potential for these connections between incipient elites to broker deals and alliances, the less wealthy have some stake in supporting these signals.

As Brian Hayden has argued, natural psychological variation in human communities always produces individuals with ambitions to wield influence, and in segmented societies generating a surplus, a few of those individuals will have material and social capital. These aggrandizers use their greater wealth and standing to bid for influence. In these incipiently transegalitarian cultures, they will, for example, sponsor feasts, usually with the backing of their clan. They amass resources, calling in all their debts and favours, for spectacular and wasteful displays, to which their counterparts from other communities are invited, always with the expectation of reciprocity. These are competitive displays; in part by aggrandizing individuals and their backers; in part by the communities they represent (and to the extent that these signals can deter potential enemies and attract potential allies, the community has a stake in their success, and socially skilled aggrandizers can exploit this to recruit community backing). We regularly find these displays in communities where there are important differences in wealth, status and influence, but inequality is not fully hereditary, with leadership positions not yet inherited as of right.

In such cases, the elites in place must claim to be brokering interaction with neighbouring communities for the good of all, on behalf of all. Moreover, that claim for common good must have some plausibility. Big Men must negotiate support; they cannot just demand it, and to some degree they must pay for it: they need to return favours to their backers and their sponsors (for a superb case study in this genre of political scheming see (Wiessner 2002b); for general overviews, see (Flannery and Marcus 2012, Hayden 2014).

These displays induce an echo: other communities signal back in similar vein. These feasts, when they went well, cemented links between community elites, as they brokered peace and some forms of cooperation, at least for a while. That cooperation, of course, quite often took the form of alliances against third parties. Thus incipient elites use their leverage within a village to make themselves the crucial links between villages, developing supra-community networks with their counterparts in these other communities, becoming the channel through which inter-community negotiation, trade in luxury and prestige goods and information about the wider world flows. These aggrandizers need wealth of their own. But they also need social capital to recruit corporate support, the backing of their clan or family. Once they have it, resources flow back to them by reciprocation, and through the economic and social leverage their networks with others of influence give them. The threat of war, the competitive and fraught relations between communities (and hence the advantage of signalling one's wealth, strength and allies) opens this door to aggrandizers to turn wealth into political leadership, and leadership into wealth. If this view is right, we expect to see inequality establish and grow where there is a serious but negotiable threat of inter-community violence, rather than where there is permanent war[8] or stable peace.

Constraints on Collective Action. In the early, pre-state stages of the development of inequality, before inequality is entrenched, hereditary and multi-layered (with local elites being the clients of still more wealthy and powerful individuals), elites and incipient elites lived amongst those whom they hoped to lead and dominate, so they were physically and socially vulnerable. Those who over-reached, who were too nakedly greedy and self-interested, or who did not deliver rewards to their clan backers, were in serious danger of being deposed (Hayden 2011). But the establishment and growth of sedentary societies (especially those based

---

[8] Peter Turchin's work on the dynamics of empire suggests that near-permanent violence tends to reduce inequality within the warring communities, presumably because everyone has to be strongly incentivized to commit to defence (Turchin 2006).

on agriculture) made the coalitional enforcement of political or material equality increasingly unlikely. We should recall that this threat of collective violence, together with easy movement, was the ultimate mechanism underwriting the egalitarian character of forager bands. In my view, this ceased to be a threat to aggrandizers as sedentary societies established and grew. First, as noted already, crucial egalitarian norms probably eroded before elites began to establish. Storage weakens support for compulsory sharing, as this is no longer an essential form of social insurance. Moreover, tacit or explicit recognition of individual (or family) ownership of land (and/or livestock), and hence the means of subsistence, was probably a co-requisite of serious investment in making land productive (and of protecting and managing herds). Second, an increase in community size and in living privately makes planning and co-ordination more difficult. Those who had a common interest in resisting elite demands (contributing to expensive displays; increases in bride price that put the poor in debt to the wealthy) might well not know one another intimately. They might not meet each other often, might well have few chances to talk discretely, complain and plan. Kenneth Ames has argued that elites increase the efficiency of decision-making in the community as a whole, for as communities become larger, consensus decision making becomes increasingly cumbersome and inefficient. Elites solve critical coordination and collective action problems (Ames 1985, Ames 1994). The claim here is the mirror image of Ames' idea: size and dispersal make collective control of elite expropriation increasingly difficult. Third, conflict has another effect that is relevant here. In contrast to foraging, farm labour can be coerced. It is not high skill, and as it is spatially focussed the ratio of guard to labourer can make slavery and other forms of coerced labour possible (often of women, whose standing often declines once farming takes hold). If conflicts lead to a supply of slaves, slaves and their descendants form a social cellar, with very few prospects of building coalitions with those ranked above them: they are too culturally and ideologically marked. Once this form of inequality is established, it amplifies other forms, as elite control of the profits of slave labour increases the wealth differences between elites and the rest.

Fourth, and critically, in transegalitarian societies disparities of wealth were not yet extreme. Incipient elites were wealthier in land and prestige goods (like pigs) than most. Those whose parents were unlucky had much less. But in these societies there were a substantial group in the middle (Shenk, Mulder et al. 2010). Their interests were not ill-served by explicit norms of ownership. They had enough property (land, herds, salmon streams) to have a stake in the property system. The general social recognition of ownership freed them from having to retain their goods by the threat of force. For those in the middle that threat might well have been ultimately unconvincing. This group might be willing to evict a particularly demanding chief or Big Man, but they would be most unlikely to join a coalition from below to reassert demand sharing and forager egalitarianism. While many individuals in these communities would have no realistic opportunity to compete for Big Man status for themselves, they would be able to extract a price for their support for one of the candidates. If it seemed that some candidate or other was on the road to success, extracting a price might well seem to be, and be, their best option. If there is going to be a Big Man, try to ensure that he owes you.

Finally, fraught relations between communities increase the risks of strife within a community: a community in turmoil risks being seen as prey by another, or by a coalition of others. While that might be a rational risk to run by those at the very lowest end of the wealth and influence spectrum (especially those already slaves), it would be irrational for those in the middle.

Bottom line: those who have done worst out of the transition from mobile forager communities to sedentary, transegalitarian communities are very unlikely to be well-placed to organize and execute collective action in response to their individually poor deal. Fraught intercommunity relations have one more important effect.

Would-be aggrandizers cannot be controlled by others voting with their feet, as mobile foragers can and do. As Kelly noted, the shift to sedentary lifeway usually begins with permanent or seasonally permanent occupation of the best, most productive sites. There is unlikely to be good, unoccupied places to occupy, either as a temporary camp or as a more permanent site. Even if there were, as intercommunity relations become more difficult, a small and friendless incipient settlement would be extremely vulnerable. The same intercommunal tensions that would make shifting to another community difficult would also make it difficult to set up a new settlement. The cost of voting with your feet has gone up.

4.3 Religion, Ritual and Ideology

Mobile forager societies are/were relatively egalitarian with respect to wealth and political power, at least amongst the adult males of that society. But as Francisco Gil-White and Joseph Henrich have shown, a prestige hierarchy antedated the emergence of economic and political elites ((Henrich and Gil-White 2001, Henrich 2016) chapter 8). Some members of the community were treated with respect and deference. That was no accident. The prestige hierarchy was based on inequalities of expertise and information, and on the benefits to the less expert of learning from the most expert individuals in their social network. As hominin life became increasingly dependent on rich bodies of information, and high levels of skill, it was increasingly advantageous, increasingly important, for novices to establish informational access to the most expert. This analysis has it that they paid for that advice with deference and with the material advantages which accrued to those with high prestige.

If Gil-White and Henrich are right, it is probable that prestige hierarchies established around artisan and natural history skills: deference went to those who were expert trackers, expert in plant identification, highly skilled in crafting complex and error-intolerant equipment like kayaks and nets. But in ethnographically known forager societies, deference is extended to those seen as having special access to ritual and other forms of esoteric knowledge. Ian Keen has shown how the gerontocracies of Aboriginal Australia are sustained by elders' supposed exclusive control of esoteric knowledge (Keen 2006), and O. Yu Artemova shows that while this phenomenon is very marked in Australia, it is not confined to that region (Artemova 2016). Perhaps this extension of a hierarchy of expertise is made possible, as Lyn Kelly argues, through the fusion of esoteric and utilitarian information. She argues that the ritual life of non-literate cultures codes utilitarian information in ways that are both memorable and precise. In her view, this adaptation is particularly important with respect to utilitarian information that is important, but not in routine use, and hence not regularly reinforced by practice (for a case study, see (Whallon 2011)). An example might be the location of waterholes in territories visited only in times of crisis (Kelly 2015).

Peter Hiscock is sceptical of the view that apparently esoteric knowledge codes essential practical information. He thinks that Kelly over-estimates the cross-generation stability of these esoteric narratives, and suspects that the mnemonic leverage goes the other way: geographic facts that the audience knows well are used to anchor narratives in memory, not the other way around (Hiscock 2020). Whether or not Kelly's suggestion is correct, many forager societies *are* characterized by real or imaginary knowledge asymmetries, and these create a platform for transitions to less equal economic and political worlds (for a similar line of argument, see (Aldenderfer 1993)). First, the prestige hierarchy lead to a social universe in which forms of inequality are both legitimate and have material consequences. Aboriginal Elders, for example, have sexual privileges in virtue of their status. Second, the vertical flow of cultural information between generation N and N + 1 is partially replaced by an oblique flow from a few salient individuals in N to all or most of N + 1. That is important, because it changes the dynamics of cultural evolution. When cultural information flows vertically, from parents to children, culturally acquired traits can increase in their frequency in generations N + 1, N+2, and so on only if they improve the direct biological fitness of those with those cultural traits. For example, if families differ in the foods they give toddlers, and daughters learn those parenting practices from their mothers, one practice will spread only if those toddlers are healthier and survive better. That is not true if cultural learning is oblique. With oblique transmission, cultural traits can spread, even if they depress the fitness of their bearer. (This is elegantly demonstrated in (Birch 2017) chapter 5). Thus oblique transmission opens the door to accepting norms and practices that are not in the best interests of those who take them up.

We see this dynamic in action in the transformation of ritual and religion in the emergence of transegalitarian societies. As communities become less egalitarian, ritual, religion and their social roles change. In transegalitarian cultures, ritual and religion become partly co-opted to legitimate new forms of inequality (see especially (Hayden 2018), while still supporting earlier functions. Indeed, in these larger and more conflicted societies, collective identity is more stressed, and the intercommunal political environment is often more dangerous, so signalling collective commitment to others remains important. That probably helps aggrandizers persuade others to contribute resources, even though those aggrandizers use those resources to build their own social capital. Yet while still signalling collective strength, doctrine and ritual also legitimate difference. In these transegalitarian communities, the religious commitments of a community came to exemplify, amplify and entrench growing differences in wealth and power. For example, it is very natural to interpret the strange mortuary practices of Levantine Neolithic, with their burials under domestic living spaces, and their displays of plastered skulls, as ancestor rituals justifying claims of inheritance (Kuijt 2008). Another important example is the feast, and Brian Hayden has built a sustained case for the view that feasts played a special role in facilitating this shift from ritual and religion as social glue and as a display of collective identity to religion legitimizing differences in status and wealth. Feasts build positive affect, especially in meat-starved worlds, even while displaying the status of their sponsors, and marking some guests as special ((Hayden 2014) pp 83–95). They are salient; they have emotional impact, yet differences in status can be expressed, more or less overtly, by differences in seating; differences in portions and portion size; in the giving or withholding gifts.

The exploitation of the ritual life of the community to reinforce difference would not be possible (or would be much more difficult) without the prior establishment in communities which did not yet have a surplus of a select group with prestige and authority with respect to ritual and esoteric knowledge. In many forager societies without marked differences in material wealth, authority with respect to ritual obligations and esoteric demands was already somewhat centralized, in the hands of a few influential elders. Once wealth differences began to establish, that made it possible to co-opt or bribe individuals with special ideological standing (or to push one's way into that prestigious set). The prior existence of a status hierarchy with authority about the secret, the esoteric and the occult, together with the new phenomenon of wealth differences, set up the opportunity for a tacit alliance or fusion between those with the keys to esoteric knowledge and those with both ambition and (relative) wealth. Thus Mark Aldenderfer writes of "an 'unholy alliance' of shamans and chiefs" in stabilizing inequality in Southern California (Aldenderfer 1993). On the analysis here, that alliance and its influence is no surprise. It trades on the prior establishment of shaman credibility and authority, which in turn is an outgrowth from expertise-based prestige, an exchange of deference for access to information and skill. That exchanged benefitted both sides.

In sum: the ritual and religious lives of these transegalitarian communities became channels through which the community is half-persuaded, half coerced into accepting the new status quo. At the same time, ritual life in these communities became an arena of prestige competition, itself a place where differences in status can be expressed. As I have mentioned, Brian Hayden sees feasts as central here. They are both a form of display and a means through which obligations can be imposed on those at the feast, through co-opting ancient forager norms of reciprocation. He thinks this competition drove the emergence or extension of farming, as the rivalry between competing families and alliances created an inexhaustible demand for display foods, which could only be supplied by early farming (especially if the display food was beer (Hayden, Canuel et al. 2013)). But farming can have this effect of supporting escalating competition, even if Hayden is wrong about it being the cause. Moreover, feasts are only one mechanism through which incipient elites can both vie for and advertise their status. Flannery and Marcus survey the ethnography of what they call clan-based societies, especially examining the role of ritual houses in those societies. Access to these ritual houses is itself a form of social inequality, for in general only some adult males are full initiates with unrestricted access.

One particularly vivid example comes from a Solomon Islands culture in which a Big Man both sponsored the construction of a ritual house, and succeeded in linking his wealth and achievements to his supposed alliance with, and protection by, a pig's-blood drinking demon ((Flannery and Marcus, 2012) pp 117–119). Ideologies that succeed in linking worldly success to supernatural support are poised to legitimize further inequality. It builds another unholy alliance between those with wealth and those who shape belief and acceptance in the next generation. Flannery and Marcus link their ethnography to archaeology ((Flannery and Marcus 2012) pp 121–152). They document a series of early Near East structures that are both expensive (given those community's resources) and which are very likely some kind of ritual centre. These ritual structures, if that is what they were, are exclusive, for the interiors were small, with limited seating, and either built at some distance from domestic spaces or were sunk into the ground, away from spying eyes. A paradigm is the early monumental structures of Gobekli Tepe. Very likely, these are an extreme manifestation of competition for prestige within a segmented society with access to a social surplus. This pattern is not confined to the Middle East. Flannery and Marcus document it in southwest Asia, Mexico and Peru. Lyn Kelly identifies a similar phenomenon in the Lower Mississippi Poverty Point Complex. This site is reminiscent of Gobekli Tepe, in representing massive investment. It is estimated that its construction moved somewhere between 670,000–750,000 cubic meters of earth (p. 194), at a cost of 7 million work hours (Kelly 2015).

In short, there seems to be a general pattern linking demographic, economic and ideological changes. Foragers shift towards a more sedentary movement pattern through some combination of storage, gardening and more intensive exploitation of wild resources. That becomes fully sedentary, with permanent settlements, if and when the community comes to depend on the full domestication both of crops and/or of animals. These transitions are characterized by (i) settlements becoming larger, (ii) domestic structures becoming more substantial as seasonal camps become multi-generational villages, and (iii) ritual buildings appearing. Cross-culturally these are fairly similar, especially in that they seem designed to be used only by a small fraction of the domestic population (iv) prestige goods become more common, often sourced from outside the local area. Archaeology and ethnography hints at broadly similar rituals appearing in communities in transition to a less equal world, but rituals that are quite different from those of more egalitarian societies.

In particular, the rituals of these demographically larger and more socially complex transegalitarian societies seem to have four new features. First, we have the appearance of doctrinal ritual: public, inclusive, low cost, low affect. These rely on semantic memory to inculcate a fairly congruent set of beliefs and commitments. These typically establish quite late in this transition; they tend to be a sign of a quite significant increase in social scale. For they do not depend for their effects on intimacy. Second, we have rituals of display, expensive by design, and aiming to attract a large audience. Hayden's ritual feast is a paradigm: with high value food, together with music, dance, perhaps alcohol, building positive attitudes towards the feast's sponsor. Many are present, but differences in status are shown by differences in role and centrality amongst the participants. (iii) Elite rituals of entry into an inner circle: consider those admitted to the inner spaces of the monumental structures like Gobekli Tepe. Within these larger social worlds there were exclusive inner circles, and it is probable that these inner circles were bound together by intense, exclusive and secret rites of entry.[9] Finally, there were rituals of intimidation and domination. Here the paradigm is human sacrifice. Hayden suggests that there is good evidence of such sacrifice from the Levant as social worlds increased in size and complexity ((Hayden 2003) pp 197–201). Likewise, ethnographic evidence suggests sacrifice helps stabilize elite privilege in moderately unequal societies and pushes them towards greater stratification (Watts, Sheehan et al. 2016). Human sacrifice depends on and displays steep inequality, in ways that surely would have a powerful and aversive impact on the less powerful, more vulnerable. Indeed, that impact might be even greater if the actual killing was out of sight, in secret ritual spaces, with those outside the elite hearing rather than seeing. Not being part of the direct audience might make the event even more threatening, by unmistakably marking the lesser status of those outside. If Hayden is right in seeing human sacrifice in the Neolithic Levant ((2003) pp 197–203), the rituals of intimidation and domination that were such an important feature of fully hierarchical social worlds (think of the whole-sale sacrifices of Central America, or

---

[9] See Hayden for extensive ethnographic documentation of the pivotal role of secret societies in these transegalitarian cultures (Hayden 2018).

Catholic church heretic burning) had their beginnings in these transegalitarian societies.

To sum up the argument of this section, the material factors opening the door for economic and political inequality were accompanied and reinforced by changes in the ritual and religious life of those transegalitarian communities. Let me return to Gobekli Tepe as my poster example here. This site in south west Turkey near the Syrian border is a massive, striking, and early example of monumental display. On this site no domestic structures of any kind have been found. But in structures dug into a hill, we find massive monoliths (sometimes 3 metres tall). These are carved with skill and precision. The site is old, somewhere around 11,500 kya, near the beginnings of farming in the area. The stone is local, but even so, cutting these monoliths from their matrix, moving them, carving them and then housing them represents a major investment in resources. All this was done with stone tools and human power (Watkins 2008, Watkins 2010). As noted earlier, this extraordinary outlay of labour and skill was directed at the construction of buildings with very little floor space. Gobekli Tepe was not a proto-temple. Whatever ceremonies, rituals or sacrifices they housed, the audience was small and select.

These status differences have a prequel in some mobile forager cultures. The ritual lives of segmented forager societies have the beginnings of role and status divisions. Australian Aboriginal initiation rituals are very structured, with different agents playing different roles (including that of dispatching the circumciser if he mishandles the initiation too badly) (Meggitt 1962, Gould 1969). But while there are agents with recognized seniority, roles tend to switch, depending on the clan, on the kin affiliates of those being initiated, on those hosting the ceremony and the dreamtime figure with which the place is associated. There is some secrecy, but it is not yet pervasive, being mostly based on age and sex restrictions. So while there are the seeds of rank in the ritual life of such communities, there is not yet an elite group, sequestered away from the laity. Gobekli Tepe suggests that that has changed, and as we have seen, Central and North American archaeology shows a similar pattern, with sedentary settlements often followed by investment in ritual structures that demarcate an elite group from the rest (Flannery and Marcus 2012). It is also true that much of the spectacular cave art of late Pleistocene Europe is found in inaccessible places with little floor space. As Hayden shows, the ethnography of transegalitarian communities in the Pacific and in Asia flows a similar pattern: men's houses and other centres of ritual, often constructed by Big Men (and organized so as to include some, and exclude others (Hayden 2003, Flannery and Marcus 2012, Hayden 2014). As noted earlier, in these ethnographic case studies, these elite ritual-cum-religious activities are often coupled with more inclusive rituals held in public spaces. We see the continuation of some of the Pleistocene functions of ritual noted in 2.4: the assertion of local identity to others, reinforcing community solidarity. But there is heavy investment in structures that advertise and reinforce status and influence difference. This indicates a major reshaping of the ideological life of the community: one that was clearly congruent with, and probably reinforced, a world more differentiated by wealth and influence (Sterelny 2020-b). I suggest that this reshaping was made possible, or at least made much easier, by the fact that prior to the emergence of transegalitarian societies, the flow of instruction about ritual and esoteric knowledge was already channelled through a subsection of the community that reaped status and material privilege from that control.

If this overall picture is right, it makes four predictions about the emergence of transegalitarian communities: (i) that emergence is preceded by an increase in social scale. (ii) transegalitarian communities emerge only from segmented forager communities, with pre-existing clan-like groups; (iii) transegalitarian communities emerge from communities that were politically and economically egalitarian, but where esoteric/ritual knowledge was in the hands of smaller, high prestige groups. (iv) transegalitarian communities typically emerge in social landscapes with intermediate levels of threat of intercommunity violence.

4.4 Conflict, Hierarchy and Inequality

An account of the emergence of inequality, and of the stability of cooperation as it emerges, needs to satisfy two conditions. First, it should explain why inequality (re)-appeared late in human evolution: in the Holocene, or perhaps the very end of the Pleistocene, if its cave art and rich burials do indeed signal inequality towards the end of the last glacial. Second, the account must be robust: it cannot depend on the chance co-incidence of very special circumstances. For transegalitarian societies appear over much of the world, independently of one another. The scenario developed in 4.1 and 4.2 meets those conditions. First of all, inequality depended on a reliable surplus. It is no mystery why a farmed surplus is an essentially Holocene phenomenon. Holocene climates are both milder and more stable, and relying on farmed product is a horribly risky option if annual variability is high. Storage foraging may have been a viable Pleistocene option. It is possible that European foragers of the last glaciation had social worlds organized around stored frozen meat, and there are claims of South African complex forager communities organized around marine resources, supposedly about 100 kya (Marean 2016). But the same variance that made Pleistocene farming too risky probably reduced the number of sites that reliably generated a large and storable surplus. Moreover, while a surplus was necessary for the emergence of transegalitarian cultures, it was not sufficient. A segmented social organization with a clan-like system was probably also necessary, to enable would-be aggrandizers to recruit social and material support, and through which that support could be rewarded. Concentration of ritual authority in fewer hands may also have been necessary, or at least very helpful, in legitimizing incipient inequality. These are not universal cultural tools of mobile foragers, so were probably not invented in Southern Africa and exported when *sapiens* left Africa 90 k years ago or so. They seem to have appeared later and patchily, perhaps because segmented social organization itself depended on late-emerging cultural innovations; in particular, very elaborate kinship systems and the deep genealogies that go with them. There is plenty of uncertainty, but the evidence suggests that the package of a reliable surplus, a clan-like social organization through which support could be marshalled and rewarded, and privileged control of esoteric knowledge, only came together with some frequency in the final Pleistocene or Holocene.

So we have to hand a reasonable explanation of the timing of the emergence of inequality. The explanation is robust, too. Local environmental factors and the contingencies of history had important impacts on just when a reliable surplus became part of life. But once Holocene farming became an option, and storage farming became more common, the enabling conditions of (i) a surplus, (ii) inter-community tension, (iii) clan-like organization, and (iv) oblique cultural transmission of ritual and religion all co-occurred fairly regularly and over much of the world. Crucially, then, the proposal does not depend on an unlikely co-incidence or a precise set of enabling conditions.

In 3.2 and 3.3 I discussed the potential role of intergroup conflict and group selection in the emergence or stabilization of cooperation as social scale and complexity increased. Once village life with transegalitarian social systems became widespread in a region (this happening at quite different times in different regions) the conditions that make conflict-driven group selection possible were present. We saw in 3.3 cultural transmission creates the basic ingredients for group selection: stable differences in lifeways between communities, probably transmitted reasonably reliably across generations, while each community is internally fairly homogenous. This pattern is more common and clearer if cultural transmission is oblique, funnelling through a few critical players in each generation. In addition, and in contrast to the residential camps of mobile foragers, surplus-producing villages are attractive targets of aggression: the stored surplus itself, improved land, women, and slaves or subordinated vassal communities. Moreover, the clan-like institutions common to many of these communities allowed them to solve high cost, high reward collective action problems, and raiding an actually or potentially defended village is such a problem.

Given all this, it is quite likely that the norms, customs and institutions of villages at risk of conflict were shaped to some degree by cultural group selection. Against this, I would make two observations. I do not think selection on groups was likely to be very efficient in adaptively shaping social practices. Second, the serious threat of conflict can re-shape selective pressures on individual choice, through changing the payoffs of individual strategies. In a world with increasing conflict, what was once an adaptive option can become maladaptive, and vice versa. Conflict can be selectively important, even if selection does not act on groups. I will begin with questions about the efficiency of group selection.

Even if selective pressures were strong, cultural group selection probably would not efficiently tune the cultural traits of a community for success in inter-group competition. The optimizing power of selection depends on a package of factors. These include the fidelity of inheritance; the size of an evolving population on which selection acts; the speed of generational turn-over, and the supply of variation. Let's suppose that cultural inheritance is high fidelity and selection is strong. Selection also depends on the supply of variation. Here the issue of the extent to which the cultural practices of a community are a unified whole, touched on in 1.2, becomes important. If sets of norms, customs and institutions are integrated, one with another, so that (say) norms about the nature of women's work are linked to bride price norms or family residence customs, these norms will not vary independently of one another. In that case, selection will not be able to (say) optimize the form of bride price that would best support collective action. Bride price will not vary independently of other important cultural traits in the population of communities. The example is not entirely fanciful. In their reanalysis of the Nuer–Dinka conflict, Sober and Wilson suggested that Dinka customs with respect to marriage and family structure norms put them at a disadvantage in organizing collective action, by comparison to those of the Nuer (Sober and Wilson 1998). For selection to be efficient, a strong form of the cultural atomism defended by Sperber would have to be true. The jury is out, but I doubt that a strong form of atomism—little to no integration—is generally true. There is a hint of evidence suggesting that norms are somewhat integrated from recent work by Fiona Jordan and colleagues on kinship, and more specifically, cousin classification systems, which vary spectacularly across cultures (Racz, Passmore et al. 2019). While there seemed some evidence that difference in cousin classification covaried with environmental factors (in particular, marriage rules), the strongest signal was phylogenetic: language families tend to have similar cousin classification independently of social organization.

Moreover, the efficiency of natural selection is linked to the size of the population on which selection acts. In thinking about the efficiency of group selection, the relevant population is the population of groups. Selection does not tune small populations efficiently. For in small populations, chance events often shape their evolutionary trajectories. In general, populations of communities will be small. In short, while I think there probably was selection on villages in a population of villages, and this section would favour norms and customs that made villages more effective in situations of conflict. I suspect that selection was not very efficient.

Second, the burden of 4.2 and 4.3 has been to argue that the serious threat of conflict between groups alters the pay-off to individuals and their within-group strategies in ways that are apt to stabilize cooperation in hierarchical societies. We do not have to suppose that there is selection on groups, for conflict between communities to have profound effects on levels of cooperation and adherence to the social contract within groups. Conflict and the threat of conflict have powerful impacts on the fitness consequences of individual decision making. The analytic and experimental work noted in 2.1 showed that unchecked defection caused the collapse of cooperation. But the agents—the real ones in experiments and the in silico ones in simulations—had individualistic alternatives to cooperation or collective action. Mobile foragers, likewise, can forage individually rather than collectively. But sedentary foragers, sedentary foragers in transition to farming, and farmers seem to have no viable individualist, going feral, option. Attempting to revert to mobile foraging (as an individual, a family or a small band of dissident ex-farmers) is likely to be a choice of desperation. They will probably have lost vital skills; they will certainly not have the horizontal network of reciprocation that manages risk; the most productive sites are permanently settled; they are physically vulnerable to hostile communities. Perhaps voting with your feet is still possible in those communities on the border zone between sedentary and still mobile ways of life, and I would predict that sedentary communities at such borders are more equal for that reason. Perhaps with that exception, opting out is not an option, and, likewise, if it is not part of collective action, open violation of the newer norms of a transegalitarian community is unlikely to be a good choice. Even for those with only a little to lose, conformity and acceptance of their much worse social contract might be their least worst option, even in these pre-state transitional societies.

As this fourth transition in cooperation developed, our ancestors came to live in rudimentary versions of lives we know. They were not yet in mass societies, in the company of strangers, and under the control of states. But the road to such societies was open. They lived in sedentary communities of increasing size; communities whose continued existence depended on specialization and long planning horizons; communities with established inequalities of wealth and power, and where individuals often interacted with each other in ways mediated by social role rather than intimate individual knowledge. The Pleistocene social contract of mobile, egalitarian foragers was vanishing in the rear vision mirror of history.

Epilogue: Why Only Us?

The last four chapters have charted the development in our lineage of a coevolutionary loop linking intergenerational information flow and ecological/economic cooperation. The upshot has transformed both human lifeways and the world in which we live. That leaves us with an inevitable question. Once defection is controlled, the profits of information sharing, collective action, the division of labour and exchange are immense. So why have so few species of vertebrates evolved the capacity to exploit those profits? With marginal exceptions, sustained, expensive and extensive cooperation is confined to the hominins. The problem seems to be with the initial establishment of cooperation. As this book shows, once a fairly modest platform of informational and ecological cooperation is built, there are positive feedback loops that can stabilize that cooperation, and in some circumstances expand it. While there is no guarantee that this loop will kick in, once rudimentary cultural learning and cooperation were linked in our lineage, it was not difficult to explain their stabilization and expansion. But cooperative niches are difficult to enter. There are, for example, remarkably few well attested examples of direct reciprocation amongst animals in nature (that is, between animals that are not closely related), even though theory suggests that the conditions under which direct reciprocation are stable should be fairly widespread. All that is necessary is that the two individuals have a high probability of regular future interaction in which each could benefit from the other, plus an environment in which help is cheap to give and valuable to receive (like reciprocal childcare).

Perhaps theory is somewhat misleading on this point. In Axelrod's famous simulated tournaments on the evolution of cooperation, successful strategies were all willing to begin by cooperating, but as the payoff tables were constructed, they did not risk much (Axelrod 1984). That might misrepresent the costs of a failed first move in many real environments. So perhaps the theoretical work suggesting that reciprocation should evolve fairly readily misrepresents the payoff structure of real environments. However, if conditions in which direct reciprocation would be profitable and stable are indeed fairly widespread, the constraints are probably motivational and cognitive rather than selective. As Rob Boyd notes, real environments are noisy and ambiguous (Boyd 2016). It is one thing for there to be an opportunity to offer inexpensive but valuable help to a social partner with whom you will have many future interactions; it is another for that opportunity to be salient to an agent, given everything else that is going on in their surrounds that is more imperative to track, and given that that agent has no cognitive or motivational specializations for noticing or acting on such opportunities. In a world without much mutual aid, why would an agent notice, care, or expect return, even though help and its return would in fact open the door to regularly profitable interactions? Even so, there is both a general unsolved problem in behavioural ecology: why is cooperation amongst unrelated vertebrate so rare? And a more specific one: given that it is so rare, how did our ancestors manage to enter a cooperative niche?

We do not know. As noted in 1.3, our information about Pliocene hominins is very patchy indeed. But we can identify some elements in the answer: bipedalism, seasonality, broad spectrum extractive foraging. Bipedalism is important through its connection to territory size. It allows efficient movement through space (eventually at the cost of the effective use of trees as refuges, though there may been hybrid designs that retained some ability to nest in trees at night). A broad-spectrum forager with a large territory has a lot to learn, and so any juveniles accompanying an experienced adult would be advantaged by taking close note of where that adult did and did not go. There was even more to learn if those Pliocene home ranges were not just seasonally but annually highly variable. In seasonal environments, and especially those subject to drought, tracking water sources and recalling the location of reliable water might well have been especially important (Finlayson 2014). These hominins needed regular water, and they probably needed it at the right time of day. For very likely one way they coped with predation was by being active in the middle of the day, when many predators rest. That both increases the need for regular water, and also makes it imperative to reach that water in broad daylight. At night, dusk and dawn, and especially in drought, waterholes were very dangerous, and Pliocene hominins were not physically imposing. (This would also select for the use of even the simplest water-carrying technologies, like empty gourds). So, first, bipedalism plus broad-spectrum foraging select for the initial steps in enhanced social learning, to take maximum advantage of the public information provided by the experienced as they navigate through and exploit their home range.

Bipedalism also selects for other forms of cooperation. One is a cooperative response to predation, by collective vigilance, active defence, or both. Dale Guthrie points out that for hominin life history to evolve, with relatively long life spans and extended periods of juvenile vulnerability, the rate of extrinsic mortality, including that due to predation, must be very low. Pliocene life history did not require Pliocene hominins to be as immune to predation as elephants, but they had to be more immune to predation than the giraffe and buffalo, both large and dangerous but with shorter life spans and earlier sexual maturity than late Pliocene hominin, on the assumption that those hominins were not sexually mature until 8–10, and had potential life spans into the 50s (Guthrie 2007). Just being day active could not have bought those levels of safety, even if they had somehow solved the problem of being safe at night. We do not know the suite of safety measures those Pliocene hominins had, but it is hard to see how a modest-sized biped could be fairly safe in woodland and savannah without both cooperation and some kind of weaponry. It is equally hard to see how these hominins could have managed without some form of reproductive cooperation; at least if the selective advantage of bipedality was the access to more resources through having a larger home range.[1] Even if Pliocene infants could support themselves riding on their mothers' shoulders, that would impose a considerable energetic burden if she foraged over considerable distances, especially if she had to traverse steep or broken ground. The burden would be even worse, of course, if she had to carry the infant. So the advantage of bipedalism—efficient movement over distance, opening up larger foraging territories—is a burden on mothers of young children, unless there is creching or some other form of support.

A second factor is the informational load of Pliocene foraging. One lineage of Pliocene hominins, the robust australopithecines, developed morphological specializations for chewing tough plant foods (though perhaps as a fallback option, rather than as their main diet). But the gracile australopithecines, including the habilines, did not. They were broad spectrum extractive foragers, typically in habitats that were both seasonal and with significant annual variation. Most likely their subsistence depended on a mix of small game hunting, perhaps using very simple wooden spears (as one group of chimps does) and gathering (Pickering and Dominguez-Rodrigo 2012). A picture is beginning to form. A combination of (i) large territory size, (ii) seasonality, (iii) significant annual variation, (iv) broad base extractive foraging and (v) potential water stress, collectively imply subsistence strategies with high information demands. Gathering in a seasonally and annually variable territory requires agents to (a) recognize a large range of potential foodstuffs, (b) know when and where to find them, (c) avoid

---

[1] Reproductive cooperation might not have been so critical if bipedality functioned to make it possible to occasionally move between habitat patches.

noxious or poisonous plants, (d) minimize their exposure in places with a high predation risk. The larger the territory, the more of this there is to learn. This is an environment that selects not just for cultural learning but perhaps even for some teaching: the costs of teaching are low; the benefits are high; the target capacities to be acquired are difficult; and errors are expensive. I argued earlier that *erectus* life styles were very informationally demanding; perhaps so demanding that cultural learning was essential to core erectine competences. That may well have had its beginnings in broad base extractive foraging in seasonally and annually variable Pliocene woodlands. The factors that made us unique might have very deep roots indeed. The first steps towards a recognizably human life were made in coping with variation, navigation and threat in Pliocene woodlands.

References

Aldenderfer, M. (1993). "Ritual, Hierarchy, and Change in Foraging Societies." *Journal of Anthropological Archaeology* 12(1): 1–40.

Ames, K. (1985). Hierarchies, Stress, and Logistical Strategies among Hunter–Gatherers in Northwestern North America. *Prehistoric Hunters-Gatherers: The Emergence of Cultural Complexity.* T. D. Price and J. Brown. New York, Academic Press: 155–180.

Ames, K. (1994). "The Northwest Coast: Complex Hunter-Gatherers, Ecology, and Social Evolution." *Annual Review of Anthropology* 23: 209–229.

Anderson, M. (2014). *After Phrenology: Neural Reuse and the Interactive Brain.* Cambridge, MIT Press.

Artemova, O. Y. (2016). "Monopolisation of Knowledge, Social Inequality and Egalitarianism." *Hunter Gatherer Research* 2(1): 5–37. doi:10.3828/hgr.2016.2.

Axelrod, R. (1984). *The Evolution of Cooperation.* New York, Basic Books.

Barker, G. (2006). *The Agricultural Revolution in Prehistory: Why Did Foragers Become Farmers?* Oxford, Oxford University Press.

Barkow, J. H., L. Cosmides and J. Tooby, Eds. (1992). *The Adapted Mind: Evolutionary Psychology and the Generation of Culture.* Oxford, Oxford University Press.

Barnard, A. (2011). *Social Anthropological and Human Origins.* Cambridge, Cambridge University Press.

Baumard, N. and P. Boyer (2013). "Religious Beliefs as Reflective Elaborations on Intuitions: A Modified Dual-Process Model." *Current Directions in Psychological Science* 22(4): 295–300.

Beck, W. (1992). "Aboriginal Preparation of Cycas Seeds in Australia." *Economic Botany* 46(2): 133–147.

Berlin, B. (1992). *Ethnobiological Classification: Principles of Categorization of Plants and Animals in Traditional Societies.* Princeton, Princeton University Press.

Bickerton, D. (2002). From Protolanguage to Language. *The Speciation of Modern Homo sapiens.* T. J. Crow. Oxford, Oxford University Press: 193–120.

Binford, L. (1980). "Willow Smoke and Dogs' Tails: Hunter-Gatherer Settlement Systems and Archaeological Site Formation." *American Antiquity* 45(1): 4–20.

Binford, L. (2007). The Diet of Early Hominins: Some Things We Need to Know before "Reading" the Menu from the Archaeological Record. *Guts and Brains*. W. Roebroeks. Leiden, Leiden University Press: 185–222.

Bingham, P. (1999). "Human Uniqueness: A General Theory." *Quarterly Review of Biology* 74(2): 133–169.

Bingham, P. (2000). "Human Evolution and Human History: A Complete Theory." *Evolutionary Anthropology* 9(6): 248–257.

Birch, J. (2012). "Collective Action in the Fraternal Transitions." *Biology & Philosophy* 27(3): 363–380.

Birch, J. (2017). *The Philosophy of Social Evolution*. Oxford, Oxford University Press.

Birch, J. (forthcoming). "Toolmaking and the Origin of Normative Cognition." *Biology & Philosophy*.

Birch, J. (in preparation). Normative Guidance and Skilled Action.

Bock, J. (2005). What Makes a Competent Adult Forager. *Hunter Gatherer Childhoods: Evolutionary, Developmental and Cultural Perspectives*. B. S. Hewlett and M. E. Lamb. New York, Aldine: 109–128.

Boehm, C. (1999). *Hierarchy in the Forest*. Cambridge, Harvard University Press.

Boehm, C. (2000). "Conflict and the Evolution of Social Control." *Journal of Consciousness Studies* 7(1–2): 79–101.

Boehm, C. (2012). *Moral Origins: The Evolution of Virtue, Altruism, and Shame*. New York, Basic Books.

Bowles, S. (2008). "Conflict: Altruism's Midwife." *Nature* 456(20 November 2008): 326–327.

Bowles, S. and J.-K. Choi (2013). "Coevolution of Farming and Private Property during the Early Holocene." *Proceedings of the National Academy of Sciences* 110(22): 8830–8835.

Bowles, S. and H. Gintis (2008). Cooperation. *New Palgrave Dictionary of Economics*. L. Blume and S. Durlauf. Basingstoke, Macmillan.

Bowles, S. and H. Gintis (2011). *A Cooperative Species: Human Reciprocity and Its Evolution*. Princeton, Princeton University Press.

Bowles, S., E. A. Smith and M. Borgerhoff Mulder (2010). "The Emergence and Persistence of Inequality in Premodern Societies." *Current Anthropology* 51(1): 7–17.

Boyd, B. (2009). *On the Origin of Stories*. Cambridge, Harvard University Press.

Boyd, R. (2016). *A Different Kind of Animal: How Culture Made Humans Exceptionally Adaptable and Cooperative*. Princeton, Princeton University Press.

Boyd, R. (2018). *A Different Kind of Animal*. Princeton, Princeton University Press.

Boyd, R., H. Gintis, S. Bowles and P. Richerson (2005). The Evolution of Altruistic Punishment. *Moral Sentiments and Material Interests: The*

Foundations of Cooperation in Economic Life. H. Gintis, S. Bowles, R. Boyd and E. Fehr. Cambridge, MIT Press: 215–227.

Boyd, R. and P. Richerson (1992). "Punishment Allows the Evolution of Cooperation (or Anything Else) in Sizable Groups." *Ethology and Sociobiology* **13**: 171–195.

Boyd, R. and P. Richerson (2001). Norms and Bounded Rationality. *Bounded Rationality: The Adaptive Toolbox*. G. Gigerenzer and R. Selten. Cambridge, MIT Press: 281–296.

Boyette, A. and B. Hewlett (2018). "Teaching in Hunter-Gatherers." *Review of Philosophy and Pyschology* **9**: 771–797.

Braun, D. R., V. Aldeias, W. Archer, J. R. Arrowsmith, N. Baraki, C. J. Campisano and D. A. Feary (2019). "Earliest Known Oldowan Artifacts at > 2.58 Ma from Ledi-Geraru, Ethiopia, Highlight Early Technological Diversity." *Proceedings of the National Academy of Sciences* **116**(24): 11712–11717.

Bromham, L. (2016). *An Introduction to Molecular Evolution and Phylogenetics*. Oxford, Oxford University Press.

Brosnan, S. and F. de Waal (2003). "Monkeys Reject Unequal Pay." *Nature* **425**: 297–299.

Bunn, H. and T. R. Pickering (2010). "Bovid Mortality Profiles in Paleoecological Context Falsify Hypotheses of Endurance Running–Hunting and Passive Scavenging by Early Pleistocene Hominins." *Quaternary Research* **74**(3): 395–404.

Burkart, J. M., S. B. Hrdy and C. P. van Schaik (2009). "Cooperative Breeding and Human Cognitive Evolution." *Evolutionary Anthropology* **15**(5): 175–186.

Calcott, B. (2008). "The Other Cooperation Problem: Generating Benefit." *Biology and Philosophy* **23**(2): 179–203.

Chapais, B. (2008). *Primeval Kinship*. Cambridge, Harvard University Press.

Chapais, B. (2013). "Monogamy, Strongly Bonded Groups and the Evolution of Human Social Structure." *Evolutionary Anthropology* **22**: 52–65.

Chapais, B. (2014). "Complex Kinship Patterns as Evolutionary Constructions, and the Origins of Sociocultural Universals." *Current Anthropology* **55**(6): 751–783.

Childe, G. (1936). *Man Makes Himself*. Oxford, Oxford University Press.

Churchill, S. (1993). "Weapon Technology, Prey Size Selection, and Hunting Methods in Modern Hunter-Gatherers: Implications for Hunting in the Palaeolithic and Mesolithic." *Archaeological Papers of the American Anthropological Association* **4**(1): 11–24.

Churchill, S. and J. Rhodes (2009). The Evolution of the Human Capacity for "Killing at a Distance": The Human Fossil Evidence for the Evolution of Projectile Weaponry. *The Evolution of Hominin Diets: Integrating Approaches to the Study of Palaeolithic Subsistence*. J.-J. Hublin and M. Richards. Dordrecht, Springer: 201–210.

Corbey, R., A. Jagich, K. Vaesen and M. Collard (2016). "The Acheulean Handaxe: More Like a Bird's Song Than a Beatles' Tune?" *Evolutionary Archaeology* 25: 6–19.

Csibra, G. and G. Gergely (2009). "Natural Pedagogy." *Trends in Cognitive Science* 13(4): 148–153.

Csibra, G. and G. Gergely (2011). "Natural Pedagogy as Evolutionary Adaptation." *Philosophical Transactions of the Royal Society B* 366(1567): 1149–1157.

Currie, A. (2018). *Rock, Bone and Ruin: An Optimist's Guide to the Historical Sciences.* Cambridge, MIT Press.

Currie, A. and K. Sterelny (2017). "In Defence of Story-telling." *Studies in History and Philosophy of Science Part A* 62(April): 14–21.

Curry, O. S., D. Mullins and H. Whitehouse (2019). "Is It Good to Cooperate? Testing the Theory of Morality-as-Cooperation in 60 Societies." *Current Anthropology* 60(1): 47–69.

Deacon, T. (1997). *The Symbolic Species: The Co-evolution of Language and the Brain.* New York, W.W Norton.

Dennett, D. C. (1993). "Learning and Labelling." *Mind and Language* 8(4): 540–547.

Diamond, J. (1987). "The Worst Mistake in the History of the Human Race." *Discover* 7: 64–66.

Domínguez-Rodrigo, M. and T. R. Pickering (2017). "The Meat of the Matter: An Evolutionary Perspective on Human Carnivory." *Azania: Archaeological Research in Africa* 52(1): 4–32.

Dunbar, R. (1996). *Grooming, Gossip and the Evolution of Language.* London, Faber and Faber.

Evans, N. (2017). "Did Language Evolve in Multilingual Settings?" *Biology & Philosophy* 32:905–933.

Fehr, E. and U. Fischbacher (2003). "The Nature of Human Altruism." *Nature* 425: 785–791.

Fehr, E. and S. Gachter (2002). "Altruistic Punishment in Humans." *Nature* 415(10 January): 137–140.

Finlayson, C. (2014). *The Improbable Primate: How Water Shaped Human Evolution.* Oxford, Oxford University Press.

Flannery, K. (1969a). Origins and Ecological Effects of Early Domestication in Iran and the Near East. *The Domestication and Exploitation of Plants and Animals.* P. Ucko and G. Dimbleby. London, Duckworth: 73–100.

Flannery, K. and J. Marcus (2012). *The Creation of Inequality.* Cambridge, Harvard University Press.

Frank, R. (1988). *Passion within Reason: The Strategic Role of the Emotions.* New York, WW Norton.

Frison, G. C. (2004). *Survival by Hunting: Prehistoric Human Predators and Animal Prey* Berkeley, University of California Press.

Furuichi, T. (2011). "Female Contributions to the Peaceful Nature of Bonobo Society." *Evolutionary Anthropology* **20**: 131–142.

Gächter, S., B. Herrmann and C. Thöni (2010). "Culture and Cooperation." *Philosophical Proceedings of the Royal Society Series B* **365**: 2651–2661.

Gamble, C. (2013). *Settling the Earth: The Archaeology of Deep Human History*. Cambridge, Cambridge University Press.

Gamble, C., R. Dunbar and J. Gowlett (2014). *Thinking Big: How the Evolution of Social Life Shaped the Human Mind*. London, Thames and Hudson.

Garde, M., B. L. Nadjamerrek, M. Kolkkiwarra, J. Kalarriya, J. Djandjomerr, B. Birriyabirriya, R. Bilindja, M. Kubarkku and P. Biless (2009). The Language of Fire: Seasonality, Resources and Landscape Burning on the Arnhem Land Plateau. *Culture, Ecology and Economy of Fire Management in North Australian Savannas*. J. Russell-Smith, P. Whitehead and P. Cooke. Melbourne, CSIRO: 85–164.

Genz, J., J. Aucan, M. Merrifield, B. Finney, K. Joel and A. Kelen (2009). "Wave Navigation in the Marshall Islands: Comparing Indigenous and Western Scientific Knowledge of the Ocean." *Oceanography* **22**(2): 234–245.

Gilligan, I. (2007a). "Clothing and Modern Human Behaviour: Prehistoric Tasmania as a Case Study." *Archaeology in Oceania* **42**(3): 102–111.

Gilligan, I. (2007b). "Neanderthal Extinction and Modern Human Behaviour: The Role of Climate Change and Clothing." *World Archaeology* **39**(4): 499–514.

Gintis, H. (2013). Territoriality and Loss Aversion: The Evolutionary Roots of Property Rights. *Cooperation and Its Evolution*. K. Sterelny, R. Joyce, B. Calcott and F. Ben. Cambridge, MIT Press: 117–131.

Gintis, H., J. Henrich, S. Bowles, R. Boyd and E. Fehr (2008). "Strong Reciprocity and the Roots of Human Morality." *Social Justice Research* **21**(2): 241–253.

Godfrey-Smith, P. (2009). *Darwinian Populations and Natural Selection*. Oxford, Oxford University Press.

Gould, R. A. (1969). *Yiwara: Foragers of the Australian Desert*. Sydney & London, Collins.

Gould, S. J. and R. Lewontin (1978). "The Spandrels of San Marco and the Panglossian Paradigm: A Critique of the Adaptationist Programme." *Proceedings of the Royal Society, London (Series B)* **205**: 581–598.

Gowlett, J. (2016). "The Discovery of Fire by Humans: A Long and Convoluted Process." *Philosophical Transactions of the Royal Society series B* **371** (1696).

Gowlett, J. and R. Wrangham (2013). "Earliest Fire in Africa: Towards the Convergence of Archaeological Evidence and the Cooking Hypothesis." *Azania: Archaeological Research in Africa* **48**(1): 5–30.

Gurven, M. and K. Hill (2006). Hunting as Subsistence and Mating Effort? A Re-evaluation of "Man the Hunter", the Sexual Division of Labor and the Evolution of the Nuclear Family. *IUSSP Seminar on Male Life History*. Giessen, Germany.

Gurven, M. and K. Hill (2009). "Why Do Men Hunt? A Reevaluation of 'Man the Hunter' and the Sexual Division of Labor." *Current Anthropology* 50(1): 51–74.

Gurven, M. and K. Hill (2010). "Moving beyond Stereotypes of Men's Foraging Goals." *Current Anthropology* 51(2): 265–267.

Gurven, M., H. Kaplan and M. Gutierrez (2006). "How Long Does It Take to Become a Proficient Hunter? Implications for the Evolution of Extended Development and Long Life Span." *Journal of Human Evolution* 51: 454–470.

Guthrie, R. D. (2005). *The Nature of Paleolithic Art*. Chicago, University of Chicago Press.

Guthrie, R. D. (2007). Haak en Steek—The Tool That Allowed Hominins to Colonize the African Savanna and Flourish There. *Guts and Brains*. W. Roebroeks. Leiden, Leiden University Press: 133–164.

Haagen, C. (1994). *Bush Toys: Aboriginal Children at Play*. Canberra, Aboriginal Studies Press.

Harmand, S., J. Lewis, C. S. Feibel, C. Lepre, S. Prat, A. Lenoble, X. Boës, R. Quinn, M. Brenet, A. Arroyo, N. Taylor, S. Clément, G. Daver, J.-P. Brugal, L. Leakey, R. Mortlock, J. Wright, S. Lokorodi, C. Kirwa, D. Kent and H. Roche (2015). "3.3-Million-Year-Old Stone Tools from Lomekwi 3, West Turkana, Kenya." *Nature* 521: 310–315.

Hart, C. W. and A. Pilling (1960). *The Tiwi of North Australia*. Stanford, Stanford University Press.

Hawkes, K. (1991). "Showing-off: Tests of Another Hypothesis about Men's Foraging Goals." *Ethology and Sociobiology* 11: 29–54.

Hawkes, K. (2003). " Grandmothers and the Evolution of Human Longevity." *American Journal of Human Biology* 15(3): 380–400.

Hawkes, K. and R. Bird (2002). "Showing Off, Handicap Signaling and the Evolution of Men's Work." *Evolutionary Anthropology* 11(1): 58–67.

Hawkes, K., J. F. O'Connell, et al. (1998). "Grandmothering, Menopause and the Evolution of Human Life Histories." *Proceedings of the National Academy of Science, USA* 95: 1336–1339.

Hawkes, K., J. F. O'Connell and N. Blurton Jones (2018). "Hunter-Gatherer Studies and Human Evolution: A Very Selective Review." *American Journal of Physical Anthropology* 165(4): 777–800.

Hawkes, K., J. F. O'Connell and J. E. Coxworth (2010). "Family Provisioning Is Not the Only Reason Men Hunt." *Current Anthropology* 51(2): 259–264.

Hayden, B. (2003). *Shamans, Sorcerers and Saints*. Washington, Smithsonian.

Hayden, B. (2011). Big Man, Big Heart? The Political Role of Aggrandizers in Egalitarian and Transegalitarian Societies. *For the Greater Good of All: Perspectives on Individualism, Society and Leadership*. D. Forsyth and C. Hoyt. New York, Palgrave Macmillan: 101–118.

Hayden, B. (2014). *The Power of Feasts: From Prehistory to the Present.* Cambridge, Cambridge University Press.

Hayden, B. (2018). *The Power of Ritual in Prehistory.* Cambridge, Cambridge University Press.

Hayden, B., N. Canuel and J. Shanse (2013). "What Was Brewing in the Natufian? An Archaeological Assessment of Brewing Technology in the Epipaleolithic." *Journal of Archaeological Method and Theory* 20: 102–150.

Henrich, J. (2006). "Cooperation, Punishment, and the Evolution of Human Institutions." *Science* 312(5770): 60–61.

Henrich, J. (2016). *The Secret of Our Success: How Culture Is Driving Human Evolution, Domesticating Our Species and Making Us Smarter.* Princeton, Princeton University Press.

Henrich, J. and F. Gil-White (2001). "The Evolution of Prestige: Freely Conferred Deference as a Mechanism for Enhancing the Benefits of Cultural Transmission." *Evolution and Human Behavior* 22: 165–196.

Herculano-Houzel, S. (2016). *The Human Advantage: A New Understanding of How Our Brain Became Remarkable.* Cambridge, MIT Press.

Hewlett, B., J. Hudson, A. Boyette and H. Fouts (2019). Intimate Living: Sharing Space among Aka and Other Hunter-Gatherers. *Towards a Broader View of Hunter-Gatherer Sharing.* N. Lavi and D. Friesom. Cambridge, McDonald Institute: 39–56.

Hewlett, B., J. Hudson, A. Boyette and H. Fouts (2019). Intimate Living: Sharing Space among Aka and Other Hunter-Gatherers. *Towards a Broader View of Hunter-Gatherer Sharing.* N. Lavi and D. Friesem. Cambridge, McDonald Institute for Archaeological Rsearch: 40–56.

Heyes, C. (2012). "Grist and Mills: On the Cultural Origins of Cultural Learning." *Philosophical Transactions of the Royal Society B* 367: 2181–2191.

Heyes, C. (2013). What Can Imitation Do for Cooperation? *Cooperation and Its Evolution.* K. Sterelny, R. Joyce, B. Calcott and B. Fraser. Cambridge, MIT Press: 313–331.

Heyes, C. (2018). *Cognitive Gadgets: The Cultural Evolution of Thinking* Cambridge, Harvard University Press.

Hill, K., R. Walker, M. Božičević, J. Eder, T. Headland, B. Hewlett, M. Hurtado, F. W. Marlowe, P. Wiessner and B. Wood (2011). "Co-Residence Patterns in Hunter-Gatherer Societies Show Unique Human Social Structure." *Science* 331(11 March): 2286–2289.

Hiscock, P. (2008). *Archaeology of Ancient Australia.* London, Routledge.

Hiscock, P. (2014). "Learning in Lithic Landscapes: A Reconsideration of the Hominid 'Tool-Using' Niche." *Biological Theory* 9(1): 27–41.

Hiscock, P. (2020). "Mysticism and Reality in Aboriginal Myth: Evolution and Dynamism in Australian Aboriginal Religion." *Religion, Brain & Behavior* 20(3): 321–344.

Hrdy, S. B. (2009). *Mothers and Others: The Evolutionary Origins of Mutual Understanding* Cambridge, Harvard University Press.

Jackendoff, R. (1999). "Possible Stages in the Evolution of the Language Capacity." *Trends in Cognitive Science* 3(7): 272–279.

Jaubert, J., S. Verheyden, D. Genty, M. Soulier, H. Cheng, D. Blamart, C. Burlet, H. Camus, S. Delaby, D. Deldicque, L. Edwards, C. Ferrier, F. L. Acrampe-Cuyaubère, F. Lévêque, F. Maksud, P. Mora, X. Muth, É. Régnier, J.-N. Rouzaud and F. Santos (2016). "Early Neanderthal Constructions Deep in Bruniquel Cave in Southwestern France." *Nature* 534(02 June): 111–114.

Jensen-Seaman, M. and K. Hooper-Boyd (2013). "Molecular Clocks: Determining the Age of the Human-Chimpanzee Divergence." *Wiley ELS*. doi: 10.1002/9780470015902.a0020813.pub2.

Jones, M. (2007). *Feast: Why Humans Share Food*. Oxford, Oxford University Press.

Kaplan, H., S. Gangestad, M. Gurven, J. Lancaster, T. Mueller and A. Robson (2007). The Evolution of Diet, Brain and Life History among Primates and Humans. *Guts and Brains*. W. Roebroeks. Leiden, Leiden University Press: 47–90.

Kaplan, H., P. Hooper and M. Gurven (2009). "The Evolutionary and Ecological Roots of Human Social Organization." *Philosophical Transactions of the Royal Society, London, B* 364: 3289–3299.

Keen, I. (2004). *Aboriginal Economy and Society: Australia at the Threshold of Colonisation*. Melbourne, Oxford University Press.

Keen, I. (2006). "Constraints on the Development of Enduring Inequalities in Late Holocene Australia." *Current Anthropology* 47(1): 7–38.

Kelly, L. (2015). *Knowledge and Power in Prehistoric Societies: Orality, Memory, and the Transmission of Culture*. Cambridge, Cambridge University Press.

Kelly, R. (2000). *Warless Societies and the Origin of War*. Ann Arbor, University of Michigan Press.

Kelly, R. K. (2013). *The Lifeways of Hunter-Gatherers: The Foraging Spectrum*. Cambridge, Cambridge University Press.

Killin, A. (2017). "Plio-Pleistocene Foundations of Hominin Musicality: Coevolution of Cognition, Sociality, and Music." *Biological Theory* 12(4): 222–235.

Kim, N. and M. Kissel (2017). *Emergent Warfare in Our Evolutionary Past*. London, Routledge.

Klein, R. and T. Steele (2013). "Archaeological Shellfish Size and Later Human Evolution in Africa." *Proceedings of the National Academy of Science* 110(27): 10910–10915.

Klein, R. G. (2009). *The Human Career: Human Biological and Cultural Origins*. Chicago, University of Chicago Press.

Knauft, B. (2005). *The Gebusi*. New York, McGraw-Hill.

Koster, J., R. McElreath, K. Hill, D. Yu, G. Shepard Jr., N. van Vliet, M. Gurven, B. Trumble, R. Bliege Bird, D. Bird, B. Codding, L. Coad, L. Pacheco-Cobos, B. Winterhalder, K. Lupo, D. Schmitt, P. Sillitoe, M. Franzen, M. Alvard, V. Venkataraman, T. Kraft, K. Endicott, S. Beckerman, S. A. Marks, T. Headland, M. Pangau-Adam, A. Siren, K. Kramer, R. Greaves, V. Reyes-García, M. Guèze, R. Duda, A. l. Fernández-Llamazares, S. Gallois, L. Napitupulu, R. Ellen, J. Ziker, M. R. Nielsen, E. Ready, C. Healey and C. Ross (2020). "The Life History of Human Foraging: Cross-Cultural and Individual Variation." *Science Advances* **6** (June 24).

Kuhn, S. (2019). *The Evolution of Paleolithic Technologies*. London, Routledge.

Kuhn, S. (2020). *The Evolution of Paleolithic Technologies*. London, Routledge.

Kuijt, I. (2008). "The Regeneration of Life: Neolithic Structures of Symbolic Remembering and Forgetting." *Current Anthropology* **49**(2): 171–197.

Kuzmin, Y., G. S. Burr and L. D. Sulerzhitsky (2004). "AMS 14C Age of the Upper Palaeolithic Skeletons from Sungir Site, Central Russian Plain." *Nuclear Instruments and Methods in Physics Research Section B: Beam Interactions with Materials and Atoms* **223–224**(August): 731–734.

Laden, G. and R. Wrangham (2005). "The Rise of the Hominids as an Adaptive Shift in Fallback Foods: Plant Underground Storage Organs (USOs) and Australopith Origins." *Journal of Human Evolution* **49**(4): 482–498.

Layton, R. (2008). What Can Ethnography Tell Us about Human Social Evolution? *Early Human Kinship: From Sex to Social Reproduction*. N. Allen, H. Callan, R. Dunbar and W. James. Oxford, Blackwell: 113–128.

Layton, R. and S. O'Hara (2010). Human Social Evolution: A Comparison of Hunter-Gatherer and Chimpanzee Social Organization. *Social Brain, Distributed Mind*. R. Dunbar, C. Gamble and J. Gowlett. Oxford, Oxford University Press: 83–113.

Layton, R., S. O'Hara and A. Bilsborough (2012). "Antiquity and Social Function of Multilevel Social Organization among Human Hunter-Gatherers." *International Journal of Primatology* **33**(5): 215–1245.

Levinson, S. (2006). "Matrilineal Clans and Kin Terms on Rossel Island." *Anthropological Linguistics* **48**(1): 1–22.

Lew-Levy, S., S. Kissler, A. Boyette, A. Crittenden, I. Mabulla and B. Hewlett (2020). "Who Teaches Children to Forage? Exploring the Primacy of child-to-Child Teaching among Hadza and BaYaka Hunter-Gatherers of Tanzania and Congo." *Evolution and Human Behavior* **41**: 12–22.

Lew-Levy, S., N. Lavi, R. Reckin, J. Cristóbal-Azkarate and K. Ellis-Davies (2018). "How Do Hunter- Gatherer Children Learn Social and Gender Norms? A Meta- Ethnographic Review." *Cross-Cultural Research* **52**(2): 213–255.

Lew-Levy, S., R. Reckin, N. Lavi, J. Cristóbal-Azkarate and K. Ellis-Davies (2017). "How Do Hunter-Gatherer Children Learn Subsistence Skills? A Meta-Ethnographic Review." *Human Nature* **28**: 367–394.

Lewis, D. (1972). *We, the Navigators: The Ancient Art of Landfinding in the Pacific*. Canberra, ANU Press.

Lewis, J. (2013). A Cross-Cultural Perspective on the Significance of Music and Dance on Culture and Society: Insight from BaYaka Pygmies. *Language, Music and the Brain: A Mysterious Relationship*. M. Arbib. Cambridge, MIT Press. *Strüngmann Forum Reports*: 45–65.

Lewis, J. (2015). "Where Goods Are Free but Knowledge Costs: Hunter-Gatherer Ritual Economics in Western Central Africa." *Hunter Gatherer Research* 1(1): 1–27.

Lewis, J. (2016). Play, Music, and Taboo in the Reproduction of an Egalitarian Society. *Social Learning and Innovation in Contemporary Hunter-Gatherers*. H. Terashima and B. Hewlett. Dordrecht, Springer: 147–158.

Love, J. R. B. (2009 (1936)). *Kimberley People Stone Age Bushmen of Today*. Darwin, David Welch.

Lugli, F., A. Cipriani, G. Capecchi, F. Boschin, P. Boscato, P. Iacumin, F. Badino, M. A. Mannino, S. Talamo, M. Richards, S. Benazzi and A. Ronchitelli (2019). "Strontium and Stable Isotope Evidence of Human Mobility Strategies across the Last Glacial Maximum in Southern Italy." *Nature Ecology and Evolution* 3(June): 905–911.

Manthi, F., M. Plavcan and C. Ward (2012). "New Hominin Fossils from Kanapoi, Kenya, and the Mosaic Evolution of Canine Teeth in Early Hominins." *South African Journal of Science* 108(3/4): 1–9.

Marean, C. (2011). Coastal South Africa and the Coevolution of the Modern Human Lineage and the Coastal Adaptation. *Trekking the Shore*. N. Bicho, J. Haws and L. Davis. Dordrecht, Springer: 421–440.

Marean, C. (2016). "The Transition to Foraging for Dense and Predictable Resources and Its Impact on the Evolution of Modern Humans." *Philosophical Proceedings of the Royal Society series B* 371: 20150239.

Marean, C., M. Bar-Matthews, J. Bernatchez, E. Fisher, P. Goldberg, A. I. Herries, Z. Jacobs, A. Jerardino, P. Karkanas, T. Minichillo, P. J. Nilssen, E. Thompson, I. Watts and H. M. Williams (2007). "Early Human Use of Marine Resources and Pigment in South Africa during the Middle Pleistocene." *Nature* 449(18 October): 905–908.

Marlowe, F. W. (2010). *The Hadza: Hunter-Gatherers of Tanzania*. Berkeley, University of California Press.

Marwick, B. (2003). "Pleistocene Exchange Networks as Evidence for the Evolution of Language." *Cambridge Archaeological Journal* 13(1): 67–81.

Maslin, M. (2017). *The Cradle of Humanity*. Oxford, Oxford University Press.

Mattison, S., E. Smith, M. Shenk and E. Cochrane (2016). "The Evolution of Inequality." *Evolutionary Anthropology* 25: 184–199.

McBrearty, S. (2007). Down with the Revolution. *Rethinking the Human Revolution: New Behavioural and Biological Perspectives on the Origin and Dispersal of Modern Humans*. P. Mellars, K. Boyle, C. Stringer

and O. Bar-Yosef. Cambridge, McDonald Institute Archaeological Publications: 133–151.
McBrearty, S. and A. Brooks (2000). "The Revolution That Wasn't: A New Interpretation of the Origin of Modern Human Behavior." *Journal of Human Evolution* **39**(5): 453–563.
McNeill, W. H. (1997). *Keeping Together in Time: Dance and Drill in Human History*. Cambridge, Harvard University Press.
McNiven, I. J., J. Crouch, T. Richards, K. Sniderman, N. Dolby and G. M. T. O. A. Corporation (2015). "Phased Redevelopment of an Ancient Gunditjmara Fish Trap over the Past 800 Years: Muldoons Trap Complex, Lake Condah, Southwestern Victoria." *Australian Archaeology* **81**(December): 44–58.
McPherron, S. P., Z. Alemseged, C. Marean, J. Wynn, D. Reed, D. Geraads, R. Bobe and H. Béarat (2010). "Evidence for Stone-Tool-Assisted Consumption of Animal Tissues before 3.39 Million Years Ago at Dikika, Ethiopia." *Nature* **466**: 857–860.
Meggitt, M. J. (1962). *Desert People*. Sydney, Angus and Robertson.
Mercier, H. and D. Sperber (2017). *The Enigma of Reason: A New Theory of Human Understanding*. London, Allen Lane.
Mithen, S. (1996). *The Prehistory of the Mind*. London, Phoenix Books.
Morris, I. (2015). *Foragers, Farmers and Fossil Fuels*. Princeton, Princeton University Press.
Mussi, M. (2007). Women of the Middle Latitudes: The Earliest Peopling of Europe from a Female Perspective. *Guts and Brains*. W. Roebroeks. Leiden, Leiden University Press: 168–183.
Muthukrishna, M. and J. Henrich (2016). "Innovation in the Collective Brain." *Philosophical Transactions of the Royal Society B: Biological Sciences* **371**(1690): 20150192.
Nichols, S. (2004). *Sentimental Rules: On the Natural Foundations of Moral Judgment*. New York, Oxford University Press.
O'Connell, J. F. (2006). How Did Modern Humans Displace Neanderthals? Insights from Hunter-Gatherer Ethnography and Archaeology. *Neanderthals and Modern Humans Meet?* N. Conard. Tübingen, Kerns Verlag: 43–64.
O'Connell, J. F., K. Hawkes, et al. (1999). "Grandmothering and the Evolution of *Homo erectus*." *Journal of Human Evolution* **36**: 461-485.
O'Driscoll, C. and J. Thompson (2018). "The Origins and Early Elaboration of Projectile Technology." *Evolutionary Anthropology* **27**: 30–45.
Ofek, H. (2001). *Second Nature: Economic Origins of Human Evolution*. Cambridge, Cambridge University Press.
Okasha, S. (2006). *Evolution and the Units of Selection*. Oxford, Oxford University Press.
Opie, K. and C. Power (2008). Grandmothering and Female Coalitions. *Early Human Kinship*. N. Allen, H. Callan, R. Dunbar and W. James. Oxford, Blackwell: 168–186.

Papagianni, D. and M. Morse (2015). *The Neanderthals Rediscovered*. London, Thames and Hudson.

Peterson, D. and R. Wrangham (1997). *Demonic Males: Apes and the Origins of Human Violence*. New York, Mariner Books.

Peterson, N. (1993). "Demand Sharing: Reciprocity and the Pressure for Generosity among Foragers." *American Anthropologist* 95(4): 860–874.

Pettitt, P. (2011). *The Palaeolithic Origins of Human Burial*. London, Routledge.

Pettitt, P. (2015). Landscapes of the Dead: The Evolution of Human Mortuary Activity from Body to Place in Pleistocene Europe. *Settlement, Society and Cognition in Human Evolution*. . F. Coward, R. Hosfield, M. Pope and F. Wenban-Smith. Cambridge, Cambridge University Press: 258–273.

Pickering, T. R. (2013). *Rough and Tumble: Aggression, Hunting, and Human Evolution*. Los Angeles, University of California Press.

Pickering, T. R. and H. Bunn (2012). Meat Foraging by Pleistocene African Hominins: Tracking Behavioral Evolution beyond Baseline Inferences of Early Access to Carcasses. *Stone Tools and Fossil Bones*. M. Dominguez-Rodrigo. New York, Cambridge University Press: 152–173.

Pickering, T. R. and M. Dominguez-Rodrigo (2012). Can We Use Chimpanzee Behavior to Model Early Hominin Hunting? *Stone Tools and Fossil Bones*. M. Dominguez-Rodrigo. New York, Cambridge University Press: 174–203.

Pinker, S. (1997). *How the Mind Works*. New York, W.W. Norton.

Planer, R. and K. Sterelny (forthcoming). *From Sign to Symbol*. Cambridge, MIT Press.

Powell, A., S. Shennan and M. Thomas (2009). "Late Pleistocene Demography and the Appearance of Modern Human Behavior." *Science* 324(5 June): 298–1301.

Racz, P., S. Passmore and F. Jordan (2019). "Social Practice and Shared History, Not Learning Biases, Structure Cross-Cultural Complexity in Kinship Systems." *Topics in Cognitive Science*.

Reid, J. (1983). *Sorcerers and Healing Spirits*. Canberra, ANU Press.

Richerson, P. and R. Boyd (2013). Rethinking Paleoanthropology: A World Queerer Than We Had Supposed. *The Evolution of Mind, Brain and Culture*. G. Hatfield and H. Pittman. Philadelphia, University of Pennsylvania Press: 263–302.

Richerson, P., R. Boyd and J. Henrich (2003). Cultural Evolution of Human Cooperation. *Genetic and Cultural Evolution of Cooperation*. P. Hammerstein. Cambridge, MIT Press: 373–404.

Richerson, P. J. and R. Boyd (2001). "Built for Speed, Not for Comfort." *History and Philosophy of the Life Sciences* 23: 423–463.

Rightmire, G. P. (2013). "*Homo erectus* and Middle Pleistocene Hominins: Brain Size, Skull Form, and Species Recognition." *Journal of Human Evolution* 65: 223–252.

Rodseth, L. (2012). "From Bachelor Threat to Fraternal Security: Male Associations and Modular Organization in Human Societies." *International Journal of Primatology* 33: 1194–1214.

Rossano, M. (2015). "The Evolutionary Emergence of Costly Rituals." *PaleoAnthropology 2015: 78–100* **2015**: 78–100.

Sahlins, M. (1968). Notes on the Original Affluent Society. *Man the Hunter*. R. B. Lee and I. DeVore. New York, Aldine Publishing Company: 85–89.

Salem, P. and S. Churchill (2016). Penetration, Tissue Damage, and Lethality of Wood- versus Lithic-Tipped Projectiles. *Multidisciplinary Approaches to the Study of Stone Age Weaponry*. R. Iovita and K. Sano. Dordrecht, Springer: 203–212.

Scheel, D. and C. Packer (1991). "Group Hunting Behavior of Lions: A Search for Cooperation." *Animal Behavior* **41**(4): 697–709.

Scott, J. (2017). *Against The Grain: A Deep History of the Earliest States*. New Haven, Yale University Press.

Seabright, P. (2006). "The Evolution of Fairness Norms: An Essay on Ken Binmore's Natural Justice." *Politics Philosophy and Economics* **5**(1): 33–50.

Seabright, P. (2010). *The Company of Strangers: A Natural History of Economic Life*. Princeton, Princeton University Press.

Shea, J. (2017). "Occasional, Obligatory and Habitual Stone Tool Use in Hominin Evolution." *Evolutionary Anthropology* **28**: 200–217.

Shenk, M. K., M. B. Mulder, J. Beise, G. Clark, W. Irons, D. Leonetti, B. S. Low, S. Bowles, T. Hertz, A. Bell and P. Piraino (2010). "Intergenerational Wealth Transmission among Agriculturalists Foundations of Agrarian Inequality." *Current Anthropology* **51**(1): 65–84.

Shennan, S. (2018). *The First Farmers of Europe: An Evolutionary Perspective*. Cambridge, Cambridge University Press.

Shipton, C. (2010). "Imitation and Shared Intentionality in the Acheulean." *Cambridge Archaeological Journal* **20**(2): 197–210.

Shultz, S., E. Nelson and R. Dunbar (2012). "Hominin Cognitive Evolution: Identifying Patterns and Processes in the Fossil and Archaeological Record." *Philosophical Proceedings of the Royal Society series B* **367**(1599): 2130–2140.

Smith, D., P. Schlaepfer, K. Major, M. Dyble, A. E. Page, J. Thompson, N. Chaudhary, G. D. Salali, R. Mace, L. Astete, M. Ngales, L. Vinicius and A. B. Migliano (2017). "Cooperation and the Evolution of Hunter-Gatherer Storytelling." *Nature Communications* **8**: 1853.

Smith, E. A., K. Hill, F. W. Marlowe, D. Nolin, P. W. Wiessner, M. Gurven, S. Bowles, M. B. Mulder, T. Hertz and A. Bell (2010). "Wealth Transmission and Inequality among Hunter-Gatherers." *Current Anthropology* **51**(1): 19–35.

Sober, E. and D. S. Wilson (1998). *Unto Others: The Evolution and Psychology of Unselfish Behavior*. Cambridge, Harvard University Press.

Sperber, D. (1996). *Explaining Culture: A Naturalistic Approach.* Oxford, Blackwell.

Spikins, P., H. Rutherford and A. Needham (2010). "From Homininity to Humanity: Compassion from the Earliest Archaics to Modern Humans." *Time and Mind* 3(3): 303-325.

Stanford, C. (2018). *The New Chimpanzee: A Twenty-First Century Portrait of Our Closest Kin.* Cambridge, Harvard University Press.

Sterelny, K. (2003). *Thought in a Hostile World.* New York, Blackwell.

Sterelny, K. (2012). *The Evolved Apprentice.* Cambridge, MIT Press.

Sterelny, K. (2014). "A Paleolithic Reciprocation Crisis: Symbols, Signals, and Norms." *Biological Theory* 9(1): 65-77.

Sterelny, K. (2015). "Optimizing Engines: Rational Choice in the Neolithic?" *Philosophy of Science* 82(July): 402-423.

Sterelny, K. (2017). "Religion Re-Explained." *Religion, Brain & Behavior* 8(4): 406-425.

Sterelny, K. (2020-a). "Demography and Cultural Complexity." *Synthese.*

Sterelny, K. (2020-b). "Religion: Costs, Signals, and the Neolithic Transition." *Religion Brain & Behavior* 10(3): 303-320.

Sterelny, K. and T. Watkins (2015). "Neolithization in Southwest Asia in a Context of Niche Construction Theory." *Cambridge Archaeological Journal* 25(3): 673-691.

Stiner, M. (2013). "An Unshakable Middle Paleolithic? Trends versus Conservatism in the Predatory Niche and Their Social Ramifications." *Current Anthropology* 54(S8): S288-S304.

Stiner, M. C. (2002). "Carnivory, Coevolution, and the Geographic Spread of the Genus Homo." *Journal of Archaeological Research* 10(1): 1-63.

Stockton, J. (1982). "Stone Wall Fish-Traps in Tasmania." *Australian Archaeology* 14(107-114).

Stout, D. (2002). "Skill and Cognition in Stone Tool Production: An Ethnographic Case Study from Irian Jaya." *Current Anthropology* 43(5): 693-722.

Tennie, C., D. R. Braun, L. S. Premo and S. P. McPherron (2016). The Island Test for Cumulative Culture in Paleolithic Cultures. *The Nature of Culture.* M. N. Haidle, N. Conard and M. Bolus. Netherlands, Springer: 121-133.

Tennie, C., J. Call and M. Tomasello (2009). "Ratcheting Up the Ratchet: On the Evolution of Cumulative Culture." *Philosophical Transactions of the Royal Society, London, B* 364: 2405-2415.

Tennie, C., L. Hopper and C. van Schaik (forthcoming). On the Origin of Cumulative Culture: Consideration of the Role of Copying in Culture-Dependent Traits and a Reappraisal of the Zone of Latent Solutions Hypothesis. *Chimpanzees in Context: A Comparative Perspective on Chimpanzee Behavior, Cognition, Conservation, and Welfare.* S. Ross and L. Hopper. Chicago, University of Chicago Press.

Tennie, C., L. S. Premo, D. R. Braun and S. P. McPherron (2017). "Early Stone Tools and Cultural Transmission: Resetting the Null Hypothesis, with Commentaries and a Response." *Current Anthropology* 58(5): 652–672.

Testart, A., R. Forbis, B. Hayden, T. Ingold, S. Perlman, D. Pokotylo, P. Rowley-Conwy and D. Stuart (1982). "The Significance of Food Storage among Hunter-Gatherers: Residence Patterns, Population Densities, and Social Inequalities [with Comments and Reply]." *Current Anthropology* 23(5): 523–537.

Thompson, J., S. Carvalho, C. Marean and Z. Alemseged (2019). "Origins of the Human Predatory Pattern: The Transition to Large-Animal Exploitation by Early Hominins." *Current Anthropology* 60(1): 1–23.

Tomasello, M. (1999). *The Cultural Origins of Human Cognition*. Cambridge, Harvard University Press.

Tomasello, M. (2014). *A Natural History of Human Thinking*. Cambridge, Harvard University Press.

Tomasello, M. (2016). *A Natural History of Human Morality*. Cambridge, Harvard University Press.

Tomasello, M., A. P. Melis, C. Tennie, E. Wyman and E. Herrmann (2012). "Two Key Steps in the Evolution of Human Cooperation: The Interdependence Hypothesis." *Current Anthropology* 53(6): 673–692.

Turchin, P. (2006). *War and Peace and War: The Life Cycles of Imperial Nations*. New York, Pi Press.

Watkins, T. (2008). "Supra-Regional Networks in the Neolithic of Southwest Asia." *Journal of World Prehistory* 21: 139–171.

Watkins, T. (2010). "New Light on Neolithic Revolution in South-West Asia." *Antiquity* 84: 621–634.

Watts, J., O. Sheehan, Q. D. Atkinson, J. Bulbulia and R. D. Gray (2016). "Ritual Human Sacrifice Promoted and Sustained the Evolution of Stratified Societies." *Nature* 532(7598): 228–231.

Wengrow, D. and D. Graeber (2015). "Farewell to the "Childhood of Man": Ritual, Seasonality and the Origins of Inequality." *Journal of the Royal Anthropological Institute* 21(3): 597–619.

Whallon, R. (2011). An Introduction to Information and Its Role in Hunter-Gatherer Bands. *Information and Its Role in Hunter-Gatherer Bands*. R. Whallon, W. A. Lovis and R. Hitchcock. Los Angeles, UCLA/Cotsen Institute of Archaeology Press: 1–28.

Whitehouse, H. (2016). "Cognitive Evolution and Religion: Cognition and Religious Evolution." *Issues in Ethnology and Anthropology* 3(3): 33–47.

Whitehouse, H. and J. Lanman (2014). "The Ties That Bind Us: Ritual, Fusion, and Identification." *Current Anthropology* 55(6): 674–695.

Wiessner, P. W. (2002a). "Hunting, Healing, and Hxaro Exchange: A Long-Term Perspective on !Kung (Ju/'hoansi) Large-Game Hunting." *Evolution and Human Behavior:* 23(6): 407–436.

Wiessner, P. W. (2002b). "The Vines of Complexity: Egalitarian Structures and the Institutionalization of Inequality among the Enga." *Current Anthropology* 43(2): 233-269.

Wiessner, P. W. (2014). "Embers of Society: Firelight Talk among the Ju/'hoansi Bushmen." *Proceedings of the National Academy of Sciences* 111(39): 14027-14035.

Wilkins, J. and M. Chazan (2012). "Blade Production 500 Thousand Years Ago at Kathu Pan 1, South Africa: Support for a Multiple Origins Hypothesis for early Middle Pleistocene Blade Technologies." *Journal of Archaeological Science* 39: 1883-1900.

Wilkins, J., B. Schoville, K. Brown and M. Chazan (2012). "Evidence for Early Hafted Hunting Technology." *Science* 338(16 November): 942-945.

Williams, G. C. (1966). *Adaptation and Natural Selection.* Princeton, Princeton University Press.

Woodfield, C. (2000). Traditional Aboriginal Uses of the Barwon River Wetlands. N. H. Trust, Inland Rivers Network.

Wrangham, R. (1999). "Evolution of Coalitionary Killing." *Yearbook of Physical Anthropology* 42: 1-30.

Wrangham, R. (2009). *Catching Fire: How Cooking Made Us Human.* London, Profile Books.

Wrangham, R. (2017). "Control of Fire in the Paleolithic: Evaluating the Cooking Hypothesis." *Current Anthropology* 58(S16): S303-S313.

Wrangham, R. (2018). *The Goodness Paradox.* Cambridge, Harvard University Press.

Wrangham, R. (2019). *The Goodness Paradox: How Evolution Made Us More and Less Violent.* London, Profile Books.

Wrangham, R., D. Cheney and R. Seyfarth (2009). "Shallow-Water Habitats as Sources of Fallback Foods for Hominins." *American Journal of Physical Anthropology* 140(4): 630-642.

Zeder, M. (2011). "The Origins of Agriculture in the Near East." *Current Anthropology* 52(S4): S221-S235.

Zeder, M. (2012). "The Broad Spectrum Revolution at 40: Resource Diversity, Intensification, and an Alternative to Optimal Foraging Explanations." *Journal of Anthropological Archaeology* 31(3): 241-264.

Zhu, Z., R. Dennell, W. Huaang, Y. Wu, S. Qiu, Z. Rao, Y. Hou, J. Xie, J. Han and T. Ouyang (2018). "Hominin Occupation of the Chinese Loess Plateau since about 2.1 Million Years Ago." *Nature* 559: 608-612.

Index

For the benefit of digital users, indexed terms that span two pages (e.g., 52–53) may, on occasion, appear on only one of those pages.
Tables are indicated by *t* following the page number

Acheulian technology, 15n.8, 18–19, 21–22, 24–25, 34–35, 37–38, 38n.17, 41–42, 50, 51–52, 86–89
Anatomically Modern Humans (AMHs), 17–18, 20–21, 23–24, 42–43, 51, 64–67, 67n.8, 93–94
Australian Aboriginals, 45–46, 64–66, 83–84, 93–94, 95n.2, 99–100, 101–2, 116–17, 142–43, 149–50
australopithecines, 18–19, 42–43, 61, 160–61

Bingham, Paul, 62, 64–66
bipedal locomotion, bipedalism, 1, 4–5, 14–15, 16, 18–19, 30–31, 113, 158–60, 160n.1
Birch, Jonathan, x, 12–13, 86–87, 113n.5, 143–44
Boehm, Chris, 135
Bonobos, 56–57, 95, 104–6, 111n.4
Bowles, Sam, 111–13, 129–30
Boyd, Robert, 40, 67–68, 84–86, 98–99, 111–13, 158
bullying, 55, 56–57, 64–67, 68–69, 76
Bunn, Henry, 62, 66–67

Chapais, Bernard, 71–72, 96–97, 104, 107–8
cheating. *See* bullying; free-riding
Chimpanzees, 4–5, 7–8, 13–14n.7, 17–18, 23–24, 29–30, 45n.19, 55–58, 61, 63–66, 93–94, 95, 104–6, 107, 111–15, 111n.4, 114n.7, 160–61
clans, 57–58, 59*t*, 101–3, 112–13, 118–19, 121–23, 132–33, 138–39, 145–46, 149–53
collective action, 3, 7–8, 11–13, 14, 15–16, 50, 53, 59*t*, 66–67, 68–70, 75–76, 78, 98–101, 102–4, 111–13, 121–22, 125, 133–35, 139–42, 144–45, 152–53, 157
cooperation, 1, 3, 7–9, 10–13, 14–15, 23–24, 29, 33–34, 52–53, 55–58, 59*t*, 61–63, 66–70, 73–74, 73n.11, 75–76, 81–82, 86, 91–92, 94–95, 96–99, 100–1, 103*t*, 104–6, 110–13, 113n.6, 118–22, 124, 132, 133–35, 138–39, 151–52, 154–56, 157–58, 159–60. *See also* bullying; collective action; free-riding; mutualism; reciprocation; reproductive cooperation
cultural group selection, x–xi, 84–85, 94–95, 112–13, 116–17, 118–19, 122–23, 152–53

INDEX

cultural learning, , 2–3, 9–11, 13–14, 16, 24–25, 26–34, 45–47, 50, 51–52, 58n.4, 88–89, 104–6, 120–21, 157, 158–59, 160–61. *See also* cumulative cultural learning; emulation; imitation; teaching
cumulative cultural learning, 8–10, 34–45, 49–50, 99, 143–44, 152

defection (in potential cooperative interactions). *See* free-riding
Denisovans, 17–18, 20–21, 51
Dennett, Dan, 45–46
diet, 1, 4–5, 18–19, 20–21, 30–31, 56–57, 70–55, 76, 88–89, 93–94, 100–1, 104–6, 113–15, 125–26, 127–29, 135, 145–46, 147–49, 160–61
digging stick, 15–16, 38–39, 64–66

elites, 12–13, 57–58, 124, 133–34, 134n.6, 137–41, 142, 145–46. *See also* hierarchy
emulation, 29–30, 36, 39–40
encephalization, 16, 17–18, 18*t*, 20–21, 23–24, 25, 42, 50
erectines (*H erectus*), 17–21, 18*t*, 25, 30–31, 33–34, 41–42, 43–44, 50, 56–57, 59*t*, 61, 62, 63–64, 66–68, 78–79, 108–9, 160–61

farming, 101–2, 124–33, 139–41, 145–46, 151–52, 154–55
fire, 20, 24, 98–99
food. *See* diet
Frank, Robert, 86
free-riding, x, 12–13, 14, 55–56, 61, 62–64, 66–69, 66n.7, 67n.9, 75–77, 81, 84–86, 98–99, 100–1, 104, 119–20, 133–34, 154–55, 157
Frison, George, 99

Gamble, Clive, 109–10
Gintis, Herb, 111–13, 129–30
gossip, 59*t*, 75–76, 78–81, 92, 104
Gould, Richard, 63–64, 83, 128n.2

habilenes (*H. habilus*), 17–19, 18*t*, 27–28, 29, 42–43
Hadza (African foragers), 5–6, 28–29, 80–81, 100–1, 104–6
Hawkes, Kristin, 43–44, 56–57, 71n.10
Hayden, Brian, 7–8, 124, 126n.1, 130n.3, 132, 138, 145–46, 147–50
Heidelbergensians (*H Heidelbergensis*), 17–18, 18*t*, 20–21, 25, 42, 57–58, 59*t*, 66–67, 70–73, 78–79, 88–89, 108–11, 122–23
Henrich, Joseph, 36, 39–41, 47–48, 49, 67–68, 86, 111–12, 142
Heyes, Cecilia, x–xi, 26–27, 40–41, 45
hierarchy, 7–8, 56–57, 59*t*, 70, 124, 132–33, 135–38, 142–44, 145, 151–56. *See also* elites
Hiscock, Peter, x–xi, 29–30, 37–38, 50–51, 52
Holocene (The Holocene), 3, 17*t*, 23–24, 57–58, 59*t*, 99, 102–3, 121–22, 133–34, 137–38, 151–52
hunting, chimpanzee, 55–56, 57n.3, 62n.5, 113–15, 160–61
hunting, human, 3, 5–6, 11, 15–16, 20–21, 23–24, 41–42, 46–47, 52, 54–55, 59*t*, 61, 62–68, 70–74, 80–81, 83, 88–89, 95, 99, 104–9, 113–16, 127–28, 129, 160–61. *See also* scavenging
Hxaro gift exchange, 54–55, 110–11

imitation learning, 8–10, 29–30, 36, 40–41, 44–45

INDEX

inter-group violence, 11, 59*t*, 101–3, 111–17, 125, 137–39, 139n.8, 141

Keen, Ian, 54–55, 80–81, 142–43
Kelly, Lyn, 45–46, 142–44, 146–47
Kelly, Ray, 7–8, 101–3
Kelly, Robert, 5–6, 7–8, 97–98, 113–15, 132, 141–42
kinship, 23–24, 48–49, 53, 54–55, 59*t*, 95, 96–97, 101–2, 103*t*, 104, 107–8, 109–11, 121–23, 149–50, 151–52, 153
knapping (working stone), 4–5, 6–7, 20–22, 27–28, 29–30, 31–32, 36, 37–38, 38n.17
Kuhn, Steven, 108–9

Layton, Robert, 102–9, 113
Levallois technology, 21–22

Marlowe, Frank, 5–6, 28–29, 100–1
microliths, 21–23, 50–51
mutualism, 7–8, 57–58, 59*t*, 63–64, 66–67, 68–70, 72–73, 74–77, 78, 82, 121–22

Neanderthals, 17–18, 18*t*, 20–21, 51, 88–89, 98–99
Neolithic (The Neolithic), x, 115–16, 124, 125, 144–45, 147
norms, 7–8, 23–24, 40–41, 57–58, 59*t*, 67–70, 76–77, 79–80, 82–86, 88–92, 110–11, 112–13, 116–17, 118–19, 120–21, 129–30, 135–36, 139–41, 143–44, 145–46, 153–55

Oldowan technology, 18–20, 24, 34–35, 38n.17, 41–42

Pickering, Travis, 62, 62n.5, 66–67

Planer, Ron, x–xi, 33–34, 78–79, 113n.6
Pleistocene (The Pleistocene), ix, 5–6, 10, 14–15, 16, 17*t*, 17–19, 20–21, 23–24, 27–28, 30–31, 41–42, 44–46, 50, 51–52, 56–58, 59*t*, 61, 63–66, 67n.8, 67–68, 70–73, 79–80, 82, 83, 86–87, 88–89, 91–92, 106, 107–8, 111–12, 115–17, 121–23, 124, 125, 128, 149–50, 151–52, 155–56
Pliocene (The Pliocene), 5–6, 14–15, 16, 17–19, 27–28, 41–42, 52, 56–57, 61, 158–61
Powell, Adam, 48–49
power (social power), 55–56, 61, 63–64, 124, 132–33, 134–36, 142–45, 147–49

reciprocation, 3, 59*t*, 70, 73–74, 75–77, 79–81, 83, 85, 89–92, 95, 101–2, 110–11, 121–22, 138–39, 145–46, 154–55
reciprocation, direct, 54–55, 56–58, 59*t*, 63, 68–69, 70–73, 73n.11, 113–15, 157–58
reciprocation, indirect, 57–58, 59*t*, 63, 70–73, 75–76, 82
religion. *See* ritual
reproductive cooperation, 1, 14–15, 43–44, 48–49, 59*t*, 71–72, 103*t*, 159–60
reputation and its importance. *See* social capital
Richerson, Peter, 40, 67–68, 84–86, 98–99, 111–13
ritual, 22–23, 40–41, 45–48, 54–55, 57–58, 59*t*, 79–81, 83–84, 88–92, 93–94, 95–96, 97–98, 101–2, 110–11, 137–38, 142–50, 151–52

Sahlins, Marshall, 125–26, 131n.4

San (South African foragers), 5–6,
    80–81, 104–6
scavenging, 16, 59t, 62–67, 113n.6
    See also hunting
sedentary communities, 57–58,
    59t, 94–95, 101–2, 115–16,
    124, 125–26, 127–29, 130–
    33, 137–38, 139–42, 147,
    149–50, 154–56
social capital, 59t, 66n.7, 79–81, 86,
    101–2, 109–10, 116–17, 121–22,
    132, 138–39, 144–45
social learning. *See* cultural learning
storage (food storage and its
    importance), 125–30, 132–33,
    135–36, 139–41, 147, 151–52

teaching, 29–30, 37–38, 45–48, 52,
    57–58, 86–87, 160–61
Tennie, Claudio, 9–10, 34–35, 37,
    38n.17
Tomasello, Michael, 7–8, 9–10, 26–
    27, 34–35, 63
tools, stone, 4–7, 16, 18–19, 20–23,
    29–30, 31–32, 34–35, 37–38,
    38n.17, 47–48, 52, 109–10, 149.

See also Acheulian technology;
    knapping; Levallois technology;
    Oldowan technology
transegalitarian communities, 124,
    138, 141–42, 144–45, 147–49,
    151–53, 154–55

underground storage organs (USOs),
    15–16, 30–32, 64–66

war. *See* intergroup conflict
wealth (and differences in wealth),
    59t, 80–81, 113–15, 124,
    129–30, 132–33, 133n.5,
    135–38, 139–41, 142, 144–45,
    146–47, 149–50
weapons, 15–16, 41–42, 46–47, 59t,
    62, 63–67, 72–73, 106, 113–16,
    125, 159–60
Whitehouse, Harvey, 91–92
Witteveen, Joeri, xi, 75n.12
Wrangham, Richard, 67n.8, 94–95,
    107–8, 113–15

Zone of Latent Solutions (ZLS), 9–10,
    34–37, 50

Milton Keynes UK
Ingram Content Group UK Ltd.
UKHW021511080124
435671UK00009B/110